FIRE EXIT

OTHER WORKS BY ROBERT KELLY

POETRY

Armed Descent, 1961
Her Body Against Time, 1963
Round Dances, 1964
Enstasy, 1964
Lunes/Sightings, with Jerome Rothenberg, 1964
Words in Service, 1966
Weeks, 1966
Song XXIV, 1966
Devotions, 1967
Twenty Poems, 1967
Axon Dendron Tree, 1967
Crooked Bridge Love Society, 1967
A Joining: A Sequence for H.D., 1967
Alpha, 1967
Finding the Measure, 1968
Sonnets, 1968
Songs I–XXX, 1968
The Common Shore, (Books 1–5), 1969
A California Journal, 1969
Kali Yuga, 1970
Flesh Dream Book, 1971
In Time, 1971
Cities, 1972
Ralegh, 1972
The Pastorals, 1972
Reading Her Notes, 1972
The Tears of Edmund Burke, 1973
The Mill of Particulars, 1973
The Loom, 1975
Sixteen Odes, 1976
The Lady Of, 1977
The Convections, 1977
The Book of Persephone, 1978
Kill the Messenger, 1979
Sentence, 1980
Spiritual Exercises, 1981
The Alchemist to Mercury: An Alternate Opus,
    Uncollected Poems 1960–1980, 1981
Mulberry Women, 1982
Under Words, 1983
Thor's Thrush, 1984
Not this Island Music, 1987

The Flowers of Unceasing Coincidence, 1988
Oahu, 1988
Ariadne, 1991
Manifesto for the Next New York School, 1991
A Strange Market, (Poems 1985–1988)
Mont Blanc, 1994
Red Actions: Selected Poems 1960–1993, 1995
The Time of Voice, Poems 1994–1996, 1998.
Runes, 1999
The Garden of Distances, with Brigitte
    Mahlknecht, 1999
Unquell the Dawn Now, a collaboration with
    Friedrich Holderlin Schuldt, 1999
Lapis, 2005
Shame = Scham, a collaboration with
    Birgit Kempker, 2005
Samphire, 2006
Threads, 2006
May Day, 2006
Sainte-Terre, or The White Stone, 2007

FICTION

The Scorpions, 1968 (2nd Ed., 1986)
Cities, 1972
A Line Of Sight, 1974
Wheres, 1978
The Cruise Of The Pnyx, 1979
A Transparent Tree, 1985
Doctor Of Silence, 1988
Cat Scratch Fever, 1990
Queen Of Terrors, 1994
Shame/Scham, with Birgit Kempker, 2005
The Book From The Sky, 2008

OTHER

In Time, 1972 [Essays and manifestoes]
A Controversy Of Poets, with Paris Leary, 1965
Abziehbilder, Heimgeholt, with Jacques Roubaud
    and Schuldt, 1995

FIRE EXIT

Robert Kelly

**BLACK
WIDOW
PRESS**

Boston, MA

Black Widow Press is an imprint of Commonwealth Books, Inc., Boston, MA. Distributed to the trade by NBN (National Book Network) through-out North America, Canada, and the U.K. All Black Widow Press books are printed on acid-free paper. Black Widow Press and its logo are regis-tered trademarks of Commonwealth Books, Inc.

Joseph S. Phillips and Susan J. Wood, PhD., Publishers
www.blackwidowpress.com

Book Design: Kerrie Kemperman
Cover Art: Sherry Williams

ISBN-13: 978-0-9818088-9-5
ISBN-10: 0981808895

Library of Congress Cataloging-in-Publication Data on file

10 9 8 7 6 5 4 3 2 1
Printed in the U.S.A.

1.

When I am inside you I don't understand
the way you understand yourself
everything else is a meadow

inside the house is coalmine dangerous
some punctuation down the heart of earth
that changes the meanings of what we do

irrelevant grammar of flowers
no one picked fall from the sky
still it's dark in here, gasses form

breath is the last community of all
learn to be a wheel is what he said
the one who at the door into the rock

wroth with me spoke and hub
a cautious fellow easily distracted
into the pit of human seeing all

the strange words we cannot live without
heat always finds the traveler, thermal inversion
over Helsinki even and the canicule appalls

rigorous alphabet of bat mitzvah
wine spilled on white satin is a letter too
but from whom and how to pronounce it

your phone won't work until you drop it
a horse head carven out of ice
every food seems to have its own religion

maniple to wipe your sweat, sudarium
that wiped his, there is a coracle on the sea
bobbing this way from Donegal a thousand years

heimlich maneuver on an old planet
let us breathe again, factor, let the light
come through the wild chives on the deck rail

let the trachea of earth ease open
to breathe that gold light in
it knows to work within the relentless interior

fractal smell of mint leaves on the windowsill
so many doors, viable release,
gold ring on arthritic toe, hot sand

the world is curative, someone wants an answer
not this, not that, wants the other thing
the other word in other words, a parachute,

Fuji blimp floats quick above the island shore.

2.

Next parapet the suicide, then Marlene
who touched me with Berlin, felt
her tight-corseted stiff white embroidered

rising through astral light a commoner
brooding morganatic hopes or just be legible
and the bees will stow their honey in it

Pythagoras was wrong is wrong, was right
in the heart of what had to be said, a fruit
like a cherimoya rich pulp and biggish seeds

to string a rosary with of incarnations
there is nothing in the sky but the moon
the sun is just the moon's imagination

earthlings are privileged to share illusion
by which we warm or rainbow
trickery through transhuman space

we hear on the radio snap crackle pop
of alien breakfasts, a star as far away
as one's own childhood sparkles hard.

3.

Less by profundity and a kind of sailor
holding flat white pompom'd hat upon his knee
while the chaplain says mass in Sardinian

believe: believe your child is a sparrow
the orchestra practices Berlioz call it rehearsing
though no one ever hearsed before you hear

deer's head over the bar in Narrowsburgh
a girl decently bikinied in a cracked pool
and then pine trees so straight

nothing grows around their spaced out trunks
love is a father too able to forget when needed
the sumptuous pneumatic blur that made you be,

a green eyed revenant at midnight
or yellow dog stretched in squalid sun
cantilevered upon the immoderate air

where hosts of phant'sies play and men do credit
the lips of visionable women there perceiv'd,
blackbirds shrill annoy'd in nearby elm

everything is here for the seeing, to be seen
bless and blue the scar marks on whose pecs
recall a mute Trafalgar far inland

kiss no one Hardy but think about their hips.

4.

as in between the go the martyrs stand
in shell and rock distinguish dark from bright
lined up before stone beehive hermitages

seeking sanctuary in the very air
a boat with no sails so swiftly came
and only there be safe from Satan's wiles

a coarse Ameriman at play
this is just an intermezzo
all music and no singing

while the story ripens somewhere else
dear god let me up and write a play
with no one in it

let your scenery and lighting do all the work
just like the real world
where no one ever says the generative word

Lost Word
you can tell the intermezzo's almost over
all over town the angry wives are waiting

upwielded rolling pin greets Harry home
had one slut aunt among the dozen saints
red haired and horny how I feared to love her

sacred difference! thou art all we kibbutzniks need
to separate wheat from weed
for ages and ages are we the separators

enough of we, so much more presumptuous than I,
pronouns are the real criminals
in this desert warfare, dead meerkats, rockets,

go running up the hill
to tend the signal bonfire by the water tower
and let them know the Ancestors are coming

soon the five thousand year long party has to end
and all us rich and drunken revelers
with all our poor be cast out of doors

when your Parents come zooming in their Lexus
and hurry snarling to the misused door
all sinews strained we hide naked in the woods

with sobbing and giggling grab each others' tits

5.

Redemption is so easy when the sun is rising
sharp edge of the air as dawn
swoops down on the last holiday

a skiff full of slaves floats up the canal
for it was a harbor once before the sand
and ordinary people knew where the world was

before the insidious calculations of the pope
hid all human life in a smoky haze of glory
heraldic with the ultimate trombone

martyrs chatter with cold
while federal grunts keep them naked
to instruct them in the tender physics of

this life they're leaving
abandoned comedy of flesh and flesh
all the pretty lads and ladies hidden in the rock

you call this documentary?
I've seen better on a kid's balloon
stretched on a wet boardwalk and bursting

from some felon's creepy cigarette
leaving nothing to look at any more
but the endless movie of the actual

and by the sea the long instruction comes
look son that wave was in Hawaii once
that breaks around your ankles now

the mysterious peril of the undertow
so many bathers sucked out to sea
forget the Red peril the world is worse

shivering monks and toppling steeples
sun hurts skin and cold hurts skin
and life is longer than the morning

straight sun or crooked sky or bands
of merrymaking girlish clouds, the end is nigh
the path through the aspen grove never comes out.

6.

Tips of two steeples clear against the sky
one pointed one squared with finials
the weird religions of Fairhaven

square god and pointy god
see them miles out in Buzzards Bay
stop telling me what the world is about

it isn't about anything
I want the pony between my legs
not just the pages of some book you read

Paulownia in purple flower now
in the cemetery by the sea
in mist the recent dead survey their real estate

for property is nothing but what is there
always around you, a kind of color
left when all the money rubs off

as "I" is what's left of "you" when you are gone
the sun is all that's left of the sacrament
the picnic in the stars when Lao-tse fell

when no one helped him to his feet he knew
this is the very planet that I feared
oakum and burlap and cinders and cigars

they build so much they have no structure left
to build themselves, what is he saying now
in old man crouch by rust-out pick up truck

engine gone, all overgrown with vines and flowers
speaking Navaho to his goats and one old toro
he'd climb up on and exit the arroyo

then at last the animal began
snarling behind the door we couldn't tell
what kind of thing he was

all noise and jumping hard against the wood
this is what is coming to decide us
an animal uses nine-tenths of all the strength its
    muscles have

even a strong man only a fourth of his potential
is why a little dog can kill you
no wonder we need walls, but why

why are we so feeble in our bones
nobody knows, it has to do with spirit maybe
we waste all our kinetic force on thinking

or praying does it, or spending all our sap
on moving things from one place to another
don't put me in your we I never lift a finger

am weak by nature and a friend to time.

7.

Photons meet gaions and the morning is,
old slacker meeting at the trough
another fisherman, I will make thee

fisher of women, who made thee?
the catechism relents
and gives for once evasive answers

god is an alligator god is a dwarf star
god is the idea of yourself as good as new again
apocatastasis and a grin in your teeth

starting out from Levittown not three years old
already in love with everything that touches
and the glory parking lot around Mondawmin

or you can touch or be a bus or on her way
to San Francisco in the morning, say, gone
for days, got married in Yosemite

she sucked the dark you stroked her long silk hair
and both were fishermen
you felt like bears in the May meadow

under the celebrated cataract
you cooked your sweet fish
now is the wrong time to remember

it is always wrong to remember now
wait it will all come back
where had it been and you were sleeping

newspapers that year adorned with famous deaths
and death means no more buying
scissor up the Visa card and rest in peace

death is the opposite of cash
the mortgage that you can pay off never
who are you talking to, pauper

this grave alone costs more than all of you
for my numbers are not known
and I was one whole life

a prince I was among the neighbor stars
and my hat hung from Aldebaran,
a door you can't see from here

I came through like fire catching on an envelope
and all the unread messages inside go up in brightness
where I tell you how much I love you and you read

elide the meanings of all the cosmoses
to those two lapwings on the near shore
dragging faux-broke wings and shrieking

everything keeps trying to recite
Christ it's like a schoolroom in Tibet
with all the alphabets shouting at once

faithless bint why won't you write
you got all the word caresses you requested
why don't you answer and say please

or carry me out to see the new moon
my fingernail too near your eyes
unfocusable night and where are you?

when the answer marches in before the question
when flood breaks levees and troops
fall back on higher ground, when hundreds drown,

when everybody is the wrong color
call it political discussion and switch channels
how many furlongs in the average heart

before it gets to yes,
no food at all or stuff like that
but all our clothes are drying out.

8.

Measurements keep cropping up
alas my lea thou dost me long
to cast my chart sans synastry

because some have listened for the tower
photonic streams to mingle in one glance
be visage and yet smile, aldermen

cannot see thee now, thou art safe
amongst the pilings of the ferry slip
one dead gull among so many books

and ivy on the wall a phantom
reader leaning on your tomb
mumbling the questionable meters of your ode

is this what you spent your life procuring
teen critics with parted lips
vexed with your syntax but along for the sex

because you make them feel a certain way
that no one does and no one maybe should
Adorno by his ice-box frowning at the Main

morning happens like the profile of an unknown woman
or a willow tree against the sky, keep the jewels
and throw the clothes away, the gates of Hell

will not prevail against thy nakedness
spirit is an alder bush, god is its sparrow
read all that in the Bible tears in your eyes

because truth takes leave of your senses
the ivy that turns scarlet in October
is new green now you stop and wonder

what color has to do with time
your hair and all that long anxiety
what does a day bring to balance what it takes away

silence Omar this is serious
men are waiting for their money
your consolations come before the wound

when people ponder what dying will be like
they have the light switch on the wall in mind
or running out of money

or pizza in the oven or a pigeon an ordinary
grubby pigeon tumbling from a belfry
and then slowly you stop wondering

who knows who knows and who cares who knows
if you don't know, right, egregious sympathies
wine spilled along the innocent,

hedonist light up your white cigar.

9.

A smile pervades the air today
call it light and talk about the photons
but nobody speaks Gaelic here

since we all guess the light you see
is just Herself at the gate below
green as your eyes and gabbling some tongue

no Hebrew you ever heard
and here she comes
the sea always trying to catch up

Hor directly overhead disguised as Ra
what do we know of the blue vowels
yellow vowels of desert sundance

a man strung up by the pectorals
red shaman crouching in green shade
all human culture one single new-forged sword

somehow got broke the hero holds it
glue me together with men's tongues
and with thy moonless menstruum

motherfold of virgin intellect bedew
the sedulous nostoc comes down to us
in us from an alien sky, one with no horizon—

then got even less coherent like sea dawn
shirred with storm clouds and the names
garbled you're supposed to cry out

at your hour in the liturgy of bed
when the knife cuts and the bull falls
forward into physics, the so-called natural world

that pillows your sweet dreams
and the gods weep to see it slumping there
on the bent constellation of its knees

all the gods but none and him we leave alone
the desert fisherman, surgeon of the healthy,
the tofu-peddler whose flute is a dry stick

still you can hear him blocks away
the plangent emptiness you wake up fearing
malevolent vegans poisoning your milk

in this town nobody's innocent enough
when a girl you've just that minute met
explains tenderly that she and only she

is your final descendant
come from the furthest future to claim you now
and you don't even have a now to give her.

10.

The sea is far away that's here today
elaborate tomorrow with iron schemes
alabaster deserts form no geodes darling

all the rest of your memories are vague
my childhood in Livonia the pale wood crates
filled with paler raffia, stone lamps

from Italy or any other name, we live
on the cusp of an understanding never comes
heartbeat below the belt, a kind of wrestling

they do in Okinawa, you think you're alone
in morning fog when suddenly a hand comes
to touch you, subway map of your skin

it all begins with being anywhere
or full of bees hiving deeper in your head
or words waddle your way from books and hush

their meaning in the tumult of their sound
you love like blankets in winter emptiness
if you say it right its thing will happen,

this all will be happening again
long as you live far as you sail
they'll always have another peculiar island

hung from the edges of the sky's apparent smile
a smudge of children playing whiffleball
no, ghosts you read about in childhood Hearst

gaudy articles soft paper lost colonies and lepers
close to you breathing up from the newsprint
lackluster ashes in your fireplace mother lost

Prussian ash heaps not one goat to milk
conning towers of dead submarines
nothing but virtue ever helps yet still they dream of agency

feckless moral code Eames chairs for shamans
the long sweet swindle of music
a glass of kosher wine without the glass

one night the car drove home alone
I would be tentative as space, I would repose
on daffy taffeta and demure dimity

as if I had a right to bed and board
meantime my luggage on its way to Oakland
I can describe only three of my four items to police

what is this one missing from my mind
but hurtling on Amtrak north to Albany
how many items make up a single train

count every screw how come we've made
a world so intricate particular
stop fussing buddy this is Purgat'ry

11.

a heron's call

Every sound is a mystery
someone dies this morning
and their skins don't want to touch

pilgrimage is easy
it's staying put that's hard
the words come in like crows to wake us

with the mind already in harness always
halfway up the horse
to trot along the bottom of the sea

but let the paper plane have words on it
little scribbles from the Luftwaffe of truth
to peck against his drowsy cheek

he's heard about but never read
like sixty thousand absolutely necessary books
but maybe this little word or two you send

can a word do good?
can it have known hell and still be here
capable of mouth?

wandering through flames the devil
tends his garden
each flame a shape of new flower upward aspiring

where Montgolfier's aerostat proposes
Out There as the nursing home's address
beyond the stars, so many propositions

so many lovelorn dodderers
sobbing among Sitka spruces
when it comes down to it everything knows.

12.

Nostalgic for agency, I miss
my soft garage, each nail
demands an implement each

tool says agency is all
where his mysteries are stored
a shelf of books is Jacob's ladder

mounting all the way to the confusions of God
we're on the slopes of Purgatory now
in sight of that ocean where heaven hides

tells us what, enough of your *us* and *we*
enough with your ocean
give me something dry and hard

(Michael is that aspect of Lucifer in charge of his fall
down through these principles of air control
by which sometimes our fire's kindled

so that the flames dance Punic letters
to be read off cave walls, black hearth
enough of *we*, enough of this or any we)

me, that jingoist commodity
I am homesick as a number
come fetch me home

relieve me of this river
this academy of trees
all you really have is vocabulary

so fall around her, follow up the slope
that shirt of shape her spirit wears
slanting towards the albedo of the summit

I could read her palms if she'd let
walk down the light into her hands
she leads anyone at all who follows

up to the landing strip beneath the heart
where information lands
ex turbine out of the whirlwind

color is her own lieutenant
I am swept up in their apparency
in engineland where I was born

fancies of rescue, fracas of personal salvation
o lift me from the Poet sings
heaven is a palace of straight faces

he always guessed but wrong again
the copter hoisted and clouds fell away
folding the tea towel neatly she explained

the earth you see down there
we see so green to skim along
is not the earth we'll land on presently,

ditch old obsession, change the name
of the one whose image goes before you
the faithless one who will not sign her name

desire is a detachable amenity
fall in love anew each day
so be more than be more be many

for need is permafrost and teaches nothing,
want is everything and keen and shows
careful written traces of its passage

plump doves walking on your stoic heart
with tickling little feet, put
the poison bottle down and apprehend

I did and thought *I do*
lost in the rotor's hasty zodiac
clatter of her engine, slept

no more narration
the easy parts are hard to write
the hard makes sense at last

takes sense and changes it
the way a mountain does by being there
doing things the hard way round

quiver on your passage home
joy leap, joy fall, a kind of music to.
It goes by stopping.

13.

Life of a bird
that's all I ask of you
the soaring stooping down the sky

coming to rest
to sleep all night with open eye
because the language is about to change again

that's all I ever wanted
a new word
and hold it safely in my mouth

and let it out
the way the bird lets itself fall
upward on warm currents over Sade's castle

when it is already there,
only then does it begin to move
to fly to where it is already—

so I would work, then, then
do some opening of your lips for you
so you can speak it too.

14.

One thing in the crevice of another
over the saddle and down the ravine
long scree slope of the flank

the idle pastoral
where sheep eat men
and the churches always are on fire

wanting something
is no more than the shadow
of what that something is

but never tell, live
in one another's shade or else to die
starfish crucified murdered by sheer light

who had been a person is now a sign
then the shadow of a sign
then the ghost of a shadow.

15.

The pyramid's shade
stretches from the backbone to the right knee
by the river, they held my sea abominable darling

as if it took men for its own
and left nothing on the bone
and fed the rest of us a stone

left the priest in every woman's chest to moan
his stupid liturgy alone
alone and never a congregation

what a tragic sound it is to "own"
like sand lifted by the hamsin wind
come sobbing through the tiles of your room

not mine I have no roof
to help me hold off heaven
the self-deceiving mortal mind

hoping for advantage from his willing exile
political and amorous and gelt
the startling unoriginality of his prose

the review concludes not unlike
a young person with the wrong idea about bananas
hysteron proteron the schoolboy guessed

but guesses feed no goats
as they said in Ithaka
and late at night the shadow also hid

no stronger than its man
poured out in darkness
a shade dissolved in shade.

16.

The sand is coming, even a man knows that,
yesterday for the first time ever
a crow was heard then seen upon the island

then another closer to the sea
the crows were talking to each other
and people knew the world had changed

when you see a crow where no crow lives
know that there is something hidden in the moors
and no one but you to see

answer if a word could say a thing
there is too much here to imagine
climbing a mountain that isn't there

mere observation unaided by instruments
on the outskirts of Weimar
tall beech trees guarding it from politics

so we can learn you do not learn
but understand instead in every leaf,
just understand is all,

the measurements are supplied to you in dreams
themselves furnished from what you have observed
it makes the images you must retain

after the savage cataract of wakings
for what we love must be sleeker than ourselves
forgetting for his moment that a star's long gone

its light has natural affinity
with the Lifeless Personage on which it falls
for light is sentient, that's the secret

and viruses are people too
so now the mystery is spread out before you
like Jersey from the Verrazano Bridge.

17.

In Attic calm a conjugation
those subtle muscles of the verb
to express all the dialects of pain

who else could make live bodies out of stone
life-sized, love-life ready, lively
countenanced, as if Praxiteles

meant to show the terrible fixity
of feelings, when mastered
by what we feel turn into gods

gods are made of stone
the stone is made of us
how strange a thing a statue is

purporting to be soul, a you?
haven't you ever come to yourself
at bay in the gloom of a museum

terrified by some mild Aphrodite there
all smile and buttock but you tremble
at the milk-pale permanence, definite

the way we're not, and permanent too
as things go, to carve a young
Apollo from a million year old rock,

art is the only blasphemy I think
mocking stone and mocking
human form at once

so we can stop and know
what beauty is
a sudden rightness in the heart of wrong.

18.

Free from answers solemnly
three hundred sixty forms of the regular verb
anatomize your guesswork

everything intact in the old grammar book
think nothing past this
these rules are Hercules's Columns—

what language does not let you say
you'll never think
but if it breaks those rules then it will smile

with incommunicable ecstasies in us
all shaped like questions
the beasts that alter grammar are Sphinxes

and in their wise seductions still
far away in childland you can smell
the mildew of the grammar book you loved

it stinks of thoroughness
and all its world is still right there
though the trolley cars are gone from Fulton Street

all the comforts of psychological analysis
o they make too much of youth
all that cute perfectibility

with such soft skin
o the nape of my neck is not what it was
that's the touchstone my fingers go by

an angel in a bar
breathed on it once too often
and now I wear my colors old

and save my shyness for the keyboard
o yare my years all skipped away
and not a cave in sight

gone like that girl from the Equator
I chanced to spend a night with once
and wondered ever after

does love have meaning, does meeting
mean, do things have meaning
the way subways have rats

always there and always busy
with their lives we sometimes glimpse
a sudden dark spot on the glistening track?

turn inside out another man's image
and find your own
like that girl sudden-married to your friend

and all you did was Dostoevsky and dawn
like the end of *The Idiot* but no one dead,
interminable post mortem on the living

grammatical analysis of her green eyes
years before Freud
and you walk by Flushing Bay devising her

wondering what if anything it was all about
you imbecile philosopher
obsessed with one red brick in an endless wall,

enough, all that is just connection
when what is needed is blue this
and Croatian that, wine once spilled

everybody's drunk forever
like Novalis tracing stamens of a lily
and tapping orange pollen on his page.

19.

By the time you get to be young you're old
children playing on the fence
you don't have a fence just a reputation

so much for you, gossamer gospel
so much for holy innuendo and whiff of smoke
frankincense the kind Farangis like to smell

to buzz their brains in crowded churches
all gold and blue and priests'
memorized ecstasies sounding like the surf

what an exhausted comparison
like the road to Thebes
on which one meets at last one's measure

green flame of sodium from time to time
as driftwood burns
Odysseus saw it far out at sea

the only kind of fire he would believe
as he trafficked with her busily
even before we came

a dictionary spilling open in the surf
that word again and all the others with it
lashed by wave and water till

she wrote the stupid book for self-protection
since what you narrate clearly and precisely
can never happen

because it has already happened, and things
happen only one time in this cosmos,
sacred law of Unicity she prays to in the night

oil lamp flicker, scent of late spring lilacs
preserved in a wet season,
will he come now, was he watching

the green flame knows
more than the yellow
but never as much as the drowsy blue

color of that sleep whose dream you are.

20.

It's all in Marx alas
or if not there in Freud
and nothing new

and nothing knew itself
in us beyond the shivering
scared and sacramental

skin of the commodity
that's all I've ever given you
darling one word at a time

in a language where everything has its place
so naturally a foreign soldier
would rip it up and take it home

walking between me and the fire
what kind of hell is this
with such lewd remissions in it?

and he answered: hell is all remission,
nada happens, nada needed,
you share a shadow with another shadow

insatiable as wind, always somewhere else
among the flarfy remnants of that dream
you call your recent life

in this place nothing changes
jealous gods and tabernacle choirs
the crackhouse on the moon

silet, he was silent, you can say it
in one word in Latin, he
she or it said nothing

drink spilled, darts fell from the board,
outside, up Apple Lane,
to ill-thumped drums the lepers come

fright night in the local mind
not a word said they
but from some the breathing was so strenuous so harsh

their gasping progress was a sort of manifesto
like D'Annunzio dropping poems on Vienna
or this weird pain in my left side

because a gasp of pain
is the first word of all
and has its rightful place

at the start of every dictionary,
aleph me no oxen,
the first word is a cry.

22.

out of the fog world and guess wrong
it's a willet with white-striped wings
and a long beak, move fast and small

low to the waves but not so low
as master cormorant's brown self
dissonant identities of men and birds

vexing each other with alternative stabilities
our Gaia is a crystal too and has her axes
down which the light that is us runs.

23.

you have to take care of money
that's the trouble it's like a child
you want it to sleep till it's needed

more like a hammer than a dog
but money is a man
it needs attention

needs to snuggle up to you
and know its dear place in your heart
your bed will ne'er be taken by an Other

we sat in Sheridan Square discerning
women's bodies through the woolen
coats of women and these women

looked no different from the women
of Sutton Place though the coats were different
and we were cold, the only warming

the ardent business end of cigarettes
cold ash moon down Christopher Street
setting and so what,

little did we know
that everything that ever was still is
you just have to put your finger on it

as, I, now, this, morning, you
dig out of that one time four a.m.
the dawn patrol of horny clerisy

still footing it beneath some all-day moon
in another country close to here
even now is then

and nothing's lost alas
though we are closer to it now by far
the No Pronoun desert with stone trees

look like ruby when you cut but nothing bleeds
and we are almost there
one more pit stop in Wyoming

the place with all the flags and penguins
the world as ordinary lie
can't wait to get to where you can't bear to stay.

24.

Exchange value infinite, use value zilch
answer: an image
aurora and her monkeys cry out to the resurgent light

every image kills
every image is Diana bathing naked
and our eyes betray us

and our own hands tear us to pieces
if you can call them hands
reach out when we see

calm down your mythography
that sounds like typewriter poetry
banged out some juiced midnight

when virgin is the only loveliness
sweet lasciviousness of all desire and nothing doing
no wonder it kills you just to look at her

25.

But we all are phantoms
Christ dancing with his sophomores
around the cross is just a dance

the best one maybe but we all dance
the phantom Real Me
dances around the me you see

and while I'm telling secrets, know
that men have more souls than one
and life by life they free themselves

from soul to soul
as now a man must loose the grip
of the Folk Soul

who makes him what other people take him for
and then the Natal Daemon of each life
must be outwitted

burn your horoscope
and soul by soul the dancers shed
all their garments till the soul

in front of you is left
and you move into that, he said,
but so many footnotes here are needed

but the angel has not come with explanations
so the wood grain has to tell us
pores of your skin when I look too close.

26.

Someone met me
like it's raining without the it
so met is like that

and it was over
(but no it)
it was a flower

(but no color)
and it fitted the time
(as the rabbit

fits the lawn)
(without the rabbit)
(leave the lawn)

when you know this much you know it all
a tune time gets around
to singing to a town

that's mode, the currency
shapes of the clouds
that particular afternoon

he talked to her till gloaming
as if she were another woman he also knew
and it wasn't that his mind was going

but that her face had come
into the domain of the absolute
where all identities blur in the sun sheen

vanish in sea light
and only what he feels about them counts
and his feelings talk, yes, he lets them

absurd imposition of the heart as news
but what else has he
to give but what he feels

when he should belong to syntax only
only to all that is possible to say
right now and not remember

the sky is remembering
something it saw we've never seen
not that we were looking, never,

remembering is the gravest risk
because we never came from there
we are newborn strangers here

and the words newborn in our mouths
no history but need
the tones time sings in your mouth

(but no you)
I think of you so much
you is the fool's name for me

the bead of water on my hand
white tail tip means bobolink
forgetting the bush it took off from.

27.

Mandrake root ripped up
laid across the path
but only the wind was screaming

the contours change
earth sinks and rises
breathes beneath our feet

so slow it takes a lifetime
to notice it and then
the old man says Maybe

I only thought
this dingle deeper
and that hill steep

maybe it was me, isn't memory
frailer than the earth beneath me?
the whole world gasping for breath?

28.

And if not this there's nothing,
a plover on the cliff
the true nature of nothing is something else

but how far had he traveled on a day of rest
the thing about him is he seemed not to need people
looked at them with mere aesthetic glance

in which no more appetite inhered
than when you gaze at a cathedral
across the square from where you're eating lunch

what do you see
inedible unbedable stone
what did he see that kept him walking through the market

if not in search of edible affinities
not to appropriate by apprehending
since perception is engorgement

and all a lie his needlessness
trotting among purple flowers like a yellow dog
seeking self-definition, is he just old?

you touched me and I fell apart
is written in his heart
in typewriter type from a life before.

29.

It all is balance musical and bird
bat mitzvah and my father
told only shyly how he courted her

faster than trolley cars longer than the moon
of course it's a love story everything is
if we can get out of the way long enough

no names, Dante showed us that,
identify, don't name, the man
with ink on his fingers told

and the police have always listened
grandfather reading *Moby Dick*
confident the whale outlived catastrophe

monstrosity is permanent he'd say
looking out to sea across the living room
while the jingle of the ice cream truck went by

I don't know I've never read the sea
enough for me a chunk of amber
resting in the socket of her throat

or far away a seacoast of chalcedony
a ruby moon with neat ephebes
playing water tennis drunk from glow

no cars on the island
but no priests either
all sin and no confession, like a bird

or the obsessive violet flowers of the alliums
two weeks have cheered
the never-aging population of some book

in which, I mean you now, you find written
such analyses as these
laid out before you even know a problem *is*

and *that* is spirit, Judge, that is what is left
of matter after the social meaning goes
an old woman crying at the sight of a rose,

30.

and then he really was awake
and water did what usually it does
arching nobly from its spout and by

its quivering trajectory illuminating
the quivered porcelain where the light plays
weary with our tricks, water bright on white

with a sound like trumpets riffing under the sea
to wash your face
light cleans your ears he thought

remember to forget
this later, the true
nature of nothing is another thing.

31.

Blue letter written on the sky
over Floyd Bennett field a silver airship glides
over kids playing ball in Marine Park

over me climbing on the monkey bars
and I have kept it all these years
a zeppelin when all else is gone

and what a handsome animal it is
its beak nuzzling through cumulus and time
to be with me here now

and when exactly is this now you boast of
camerado, chair arm sophophilist
that yellow thing up there a glue

a screw? to hold the sky together
so your dirigible can float
gold? not gold?

words are coins and nothing else
candles are sparrows
night is just the sky fallen down around us

trailing lightless corridors of deep space
autopsy table
dark inside the torso the young man

peeled open blood eagle
the things that we examine
the foundering raft the septic lung

all coins, for everything is money
a system hard against your skin
held like another person's hand.

32.

See photograph attached
of their white colonies
leprous on the beachy rock

this cross that moon these barnacles
and that one, this mirror,
Horace's town whose name won't fit his meter

that cross this moon this mirror
those horns on the bull skull
to leap over, jump over the mirror

the other child not Minos' but Pasiphae's
boy cow jumped over the moon
kicks it as she passes

becomes the sun, Bruno burns,
the shells of a princess tree
have tiny seeds a-plenty

tiny whitish from the pale brown fall
over the May lawn under purple flowers
and no leaves yet

pecans of Sodom, the cow
never came back
we see her horns in every temple

and her stall or throne on which
some Christian bishop blasphemously sits
but I have seen her on a stormy day

come calmly from the east
humaniform and dry mid all the hurricanes
reproaching me for casual attire

for I had worn language to our tryst,
fierce she peeled the letters off me one by one
till I had barebone words

unwriteable, unsayable
and these she took and wove a skin
for both of us to share

till the chill night had passed
and sunlight crept nervous down her path
and I still didn't understand and never will.

33.

you're thinking like a barnacle she said
clinging to the thing you thought
but thinking and forgetting in the same instant

that is the freedom of the storm at sea
let go and let it go
you try to memorize the seagull's cry

her shoes are near me on the sand
drenched, half full of ocean
thank god for the thingliness of things

who is this you're thanking now
always some aggressive ontology
reifying gratitude into some misty donor of

whatever it is you're grateful for
no I thank the roof for no more rain
I thank the rain for no more heat of day

I call this thanking my theology
I learned it down the worn stone stairs
to the cave where Abraham is buried

tomb in Machpelah with a crucifix
above the door as Benjamin reported
shocked to see it on his way in

you are no scholar I perceive
for Abraham is living yet
look at me here I am

I am the one who says you
when you say listen to me
and I do and I will and the cross that bothers you

is only a piece of my mirror
look in the glass and remember your face
you will need it someday

when I call you by some other name
you'll need the cow and her bull
high elm trees by his Tiber with fish in them

and the fish still living
and the river turning upside down
the moon gives lovely light but not enough to see.

34.

Rain mind sea throes of tree
my mother and my father are calling me
on some weird cell phone

a ring inside me amplified by rain
current induction resistance
hear us we have one voice now

welded wielded in you
all morning I hear the phone ringing
can't find it keep hearing

strange ring tone of the dead
have no voice now
I need to hear them

I think it started when I heard
the wind shrill around the uprooted root
mandrake, Blueberry Hill,

and thought of the long wet street in Hudson
past the Jamaican chophouse to the river
this rain has been everywhere that touches me now

only the temperature changes
water is the same as remembering
mother father who are you now

the ring tone tune the Snowy
Breasted Pearl the part where it sings
alone alone alone I hear your faces in the rain

the words are plain this year
plain enough to mystify
old roadmap stuffed beside the driver's seat

so who was this famous passenger
we were driving to Emmaus
where we're always going

out for a Sunday spin
dinner at Patricia Murphy's then this long drive
with a perfectly ordinary looking incarnate god

beside me, braking for gas just as the evening climbed
deep-clouded up the eastern sky
windowed with gold remembrances from across the earth

what can I say to my father what could I tell
my mother we drove in silence I was always
talking I am trying to explain it to them even now.

35.

And there it was all round us
sepia and squid
a new and better sea, a pagan flood

we swim or sail or drown in what we made
the astonishing emanation of us, of our salt
we made language the way god made the world

poetry is language sitting around
gossiping about its family
talking drunk or sober always about itself

because as the sophophilers explained
all that language really
understands is language

all it can talk about is self
maybe itself or maybe another self
but never the actual selfless other

the thing attended to, the grail out there
here where we have come
flapping our hands like exhausted eunuchs

wondering what turn of the cloth is left
to puzzle our cunning fingers
before the naked empress stands alone

simple with light, an ordinary morning.
The habits of have
don't sweat the narrative details

we don't see anything when you say naked
and there are no ordinary mornings
except in Cambridge once

walking catercorner cross Parkers Piece I understood
this is all just exactly as it is
only I'm not here, I'm the expendable

element, this is the actual,
it can't be ordinary where I am,
not from any specialness I have but from appetite

I suck the seen world deep into myself
except that once, the one
indigestible suchness of an ordinary place I yearn for still

maybe that's why we finally do die
to visit the most exotic place of all
the island with no me on it

just everything being as it is
death's agency arranges one-way flight
but even she can make no promises

since Adam's housecat ran away
and she neglects to operate
busying the surgery for our final gender.

36.

life is one sex
death another
but not the other

and no reason
to die to get there
"living, I want to depart   D.H.L.

to where I am" not,
that is the journey
to get there living

and still see the yellow
of the everlasting rose
and smell it too

which Dante never
admits he does or did
but imagine it

fragrance of June
rose size of the sky
when even now at noon

we stop at the boulder among roses
to talk, a talk stone
where the cellphone works

far mainland
goddess of traffic
I found this fetish

underneath the breast bone
tell time for me, tell time
to come for me

time's in a woman
her hands,
no warrior understands a clock

no clock tells time
and not that bright shield
spun across the sky

so enamored with going down
Hel's bridge to that island
where they drink the milk of steel

and sew their fingers
to the pommel of the sword
and sleep in fire

try to escape from logic
supply demand the market's leery
the school bell rings

everything happens when we make sense.

37.

(Sunday in the park)
(the light from the lamp
falling on the failed poem)

(an ordinary evening)
never let the poor woman rest
feet all day back all night

salt and urine
a slip of god's tongue
truth is a horizon

and beyond it neither true nor false
only the unremembered
indescribable where she comes from

in Italy people call her Verità
but what do people know
only their shapes make sense

only their skin is true
where beauty lives
molecule-thick layer of philosophy.

38.

Pale flag of someone's otherness
I taste on the island wind
wantless in gazing

mousetrapped in memory again
ridiculous as usual, seagull in a golf cart
or trying to speak French

roses to think about: postulation
what a sophophiler does
or baby nun declaring her identity

provisional as an argument of will
before the altar
Pascal must have knelt at too

stringing words together
to say what is it feels
that humming in his head

sounds like an ancient romance
he read as a child, Roland's horn
calls far away the kill

but he doesn't know how to die,
philosophy is infant sex
because philosophy has no *other*

that is its consolation
everything that can be thought is true
enough to think it.

39.

What is worrying you
this grumbled morning?
smokestacks of the mainland

when I climb the hill I see far off
the coastline of America
wandering island

nomads have tribes
but I have only *this*
haecceity he said

the definition of this
has been the chief work of philosophers in recent days
say since Cusanus bathed in the Adige

its quick cold waters anxious for a south
he guessed was made up richly
of a million thisses splendent in the sun

and sheep nearby and nightingales
and untouched shepherdesses with their songs
and where such music was

you'd find your *this*
not far from goat and olive
where folk eat cheese and bread

and unashamedly say prayers to the Moon
calling her Mother of God Our Lady
who takes all fear away

that's why they say the moon is made
of green cheese
because her great light is domestic light

our light, mother light, nourishing and guide
smiling home light full tonight
above this sea you hate me to discuss.

40.

what makes a thing go on
or makes it think what it is thinking
or makes it think

that what it's thinking
is worth thinking
out loud and to some other

a girl say quiet among shadow
of a ruined abbey
purple flowers small in the stone cracks

or mortarless ashlars of the mind
because the mind is always ruined
to begin with, roofless,

a court of owls and crows
open to blue heaven
the mind is a great shipwreck

and she's walking round the ruins
blessing herself from the dry
holy water stoup the broken font

and he wants to think at her
think his thinking her way
till she hears him

only if thinking gets all the way
over to her, can thinking really think
not just wander

ruined in ruinless shade
not even a broken wall
to call its own

some skin
the think-thing
thing thinks in him

skin wander
lust and starry night
the whole world indoors

tea stain on the white towel
that's it at last, the map
of his original country

the road he'd been following
all those persons all that skin
to find this one

he wanted to say something
to you about you
a preposition is a proposition

the devil's golden chain
linked from ear to ear
not what we say but what we hear.

41.

From dream to dream
it moves, call it history
those spaces in between

who made you cry out in your sleep
all the words clear, meaningless
but no names, just like now

build a whole life that way
with no names, a ship
to get away from your life

a ship from Travemünde
into the mild Baltic
frozen a hundred meters out from shore

all that we can remember
is weather, and architecture
is the permanent climate of our space

people shadows in cathedrals
bus depots and esplanades
no wonder Ensor saw only masks around the Man

it's our fault not theirs
we can barely see, we don't remember
only the faces that we shouldn't

who stare at us impassive in the dream
in reverie the faces
we studied too long or feared too much

just clouds now overhead
just fatuous resemblances
pale marks on dark meat my mothers

the sound of someone knowing something.

42.

A scream a wordless feeling is
let language do its work
silence is evidence

word hides mind
so you pass uninterpreted
through the chattering street

what other hideout have you but the heart
so few words the heart can hear
even then you'll never tell

the sun at midnight you see shining
risen in your body
whenever you think this, or that.

43.

certain images
do not leave alone
the cellar stairs

off the hallway
keep latched at night
or Bruno burning

who's down there
into the February sky
so many years

memory
is a mistranslation
of what never happened

could have happened,
the world itself
a mistranslation of a lost original,

intention like a bird into the empty
sky's vast code
finding her way home

or not, being non-recursive,
lost
like Whitman's seabird

that is not a word
it's sunlight on the water
and a wing lifting through it

a wave he said
not a thing you know
just a behavior

as even you one day might smile
to see a miller come all guano white
from his hard work

and the smile would belong to neither
like the acrobat's smile that Rilke
wanted to bottle and label and dispense

a chemical of joy
like the pigeons whirling through
the gritty smoke of Bruno burning

the words are stones
rubble from the torn-down houses
of exiled countesses

has it never been explained to you
that reading a book is a violation
savages squatting in a great palazzo

camping, shitting on the floor,
campfire in the great salon,
sleeping anywhere?

a reader lives in a book that way
attentive only to his own needs
impoverished appetite and meager understanding

never guessing how the bell-pull works
or what god the dumbwaiter serves
or how to use the tantalus or microwave

yet it's all around him
even in the least of books
a wilderness of missed connections

even the best reader is the worst translator
missing the point of everything
being literal at the wrong moment

hinting profundities when all the author meant
was cellar door and cellar stairs
down to the abandoned coal bin

where as a child he said and read
books just like this and kept the demons off
with one small lamp,

light is like a map
the word it shows
a lost river off the Amazon and never come home

to that thick Greek Grammar saved his life
night after night
when the spooks walked out of his head and lurked

soft as silverfish in cellar dust
since grammar seemed the safest art
no monsters vex a conjugating scholar

and Mahler hums on the record changer
disk after disk dropping to continue
the ever-shimmering blue of distances receding

it is the only story he knows worth telling
the distances the tune of separation
the way a mirror is obsessed

with the momentary face
that stares into it wide-eyed with self-analysis
but what if a mirror could remember

or the sky remember every one of us
and Bruno be with god
and clowns run through the street

hammering people with balloons
shaking their rattles like rain in the jungle
but no water just the flame around the stake

stay in the long place the long belonging
the ordinary the tissue and the closet
sometimes the fireplace the kitchen sink

one bends over it to wash the dark green leaves
of feldsalat, one bends lower to examine
a suspect leaf and as one bends

one is also being scrutinized
the air has eyes you know
the wind has quiet fingers

they try to understand you deep
why everything is green,
who taught us to do these things with our skin.

44.

"Most of the natives
live in fear of our trombones.
This is physical not psychological

they wonder how we can bear
what brass does to their ears
the 'voice of bright stone'

that hurts them so
they fall and welter when we play
the meekest reveille,

bright stone is any metal
tin as much as gold
they go to sleep as soon as it's dark"

 "Arthritis in the finger joints
goes with a fear of snakes—
what dexterity they gave up

to win mere lissomeness—
Every animal is an abandonment."
A hell. Hear him, a voice has arms,

something is stirring in the world
the stars round up in a circle
and stand like stones

menhirs Renoir's *Toni* 1931
how black the black how white the sun
the wind takes shelter here

wake up now, whitecaps, wake
safe in the skirts of your dubious desire
no sail on the sound

it's all about conflict
every voice conflicts with every other
but this is Dasein stuff

conflict with nothing at stake
just the right to disagree
and hope from all that lucency of sense

pronoun wrangling with pronoun some
better thing than goal will come
a revolution with no ifs in it

"Dark hedges by the power station
the path so narrow
the snake can hardly slip along it

any face could be looking from the leaves
goat face with human eyes
or any face at all the glass remembers

existential conflict
atheist theologians at each other's throats
dreamers dueling in their dream."

45.

Hackers had recovered everything
anybody had ever thought
trapped in the elegant machine

still clear as cuneiform—
once thinking goes into language
it is locked in the world

and nothing can be lost
language feeds on itself
writing is practical

you stick it in
you wedge the clay apart and leave
its lips gaping with significance

lips of the wound made to speak
because once a thing is said
it can never be unspoken

cuneiform lasts as long as weather does
that's what they're trying to tell you
about your monumental hard drive

terabytes of permanence
awaiting centuries of indifference
bravely your mind

is a skylight in an old museum
over the Assyrian sculpture
or vast gallery where arms and armor teach

tepid knights and knightesses today
to lick cold steel
and then the winter light falls down

all the historiated tapestries rustle in your head
if that is where the mind is stored
nobody ever knew exactly

somewhere between the hard drive and the sea
can't you forget the sea
I can't forget anything that's why you love me

sometimes, the weird dyslexias of desire
liebeshass and after Mass
you squeezed against me in the galilee

and all night long of course we dream
of you who isn't you
being sweet to me who is not me

(Sunday in the park, the language)
they still speak Latin on this island
sea fog shifting through the Catholic dead

the gleam of everything contradicts all loss
see it is written and stays written
a mouth opens and says it wherever you look

the mind congested with its own simplicity
around the corner where she waits
and waiting's all the make up she needs

the air of expectancy
be it done to me according to thy word
always that word, the meta-thing

the narcissist in the mouth
gaze at the sound in your lips
and try to get the mirror to forget

make sense between us not outside
tell me why all the Catholics died
tell me who the ghosts all are

they were the lepers on Penikese
the island always next door
lucky for us that ghosts can't swim

their names are on a single monument
all their nationalities are named
a stone that does your memory for you

once you let the name inside the stone
something written in
the mind stays in the world.

46.

I can't forget the smile though I forget its girl
(Sunday in the woman walk the beach)
banks of the Moldau turret window

opens someone falls
this is not his body
this is my body

gnomic dreams in Hartford
you were born there the language
changing rapidly you slept your way to.

47.

Embedded song
lyrical reporters
trapped in the battle they essay to describe

wounded with news
as if a definition of the art
or those who practice it,

sine wave signal generator
tone given off by the machine
embedded ear

and in the bushes behind the Masonic temple
all the Friday nights that ever were
barfing up avowals

tawdry ecstasies
lying confessions lyrical
the sun at midnight

all I'm good for
but the animal I ride
this wooden horse with clever tongue

that's grammar that's the diff
you make a mark
along the bark of sycamore

then try a generation later to tell
it from the natural expression of
such a moody tree

how can you with such short breath
begin to translate the whims of wood
angels out of work

then the crow the cuff the chariot the ha ha of horses
the acronyms of war
armies shun the simple names of things

maybe shame keeps them from calling
a gun a gun or a casualty a dead child
maybe they know if they hurt language first

all the other victims will die quicker
and those who kill them won't
have a clue to what they've done

but nobody knows
and nobody knows nobody knows but me
I am the candle that lights without flame

the wolf you never have to feed
the fireman who lives in the fire
the Baltic schooner that needs no sea

o your precious sea again
mother of irony our lady
so hard to let the word just say

we get so nervous around language
first thing you know you'll be thinking
or counting sounds like Jakobson

such strange houses a poem builds
all windows and no doors
a monkey face at every window.

48.

Nothing to do with your art career
the world gives you what you need
say to it lucidly You owe me nothing

I came here for my own pleasure
let me share it with you
like Epictetus fruit trees and no blame

while in the Holy Land pee on the ground
to bring back your feeble golden river to its source
like a woman looking up a word in a lexicon

and you love her too
why not she stepped boldly
out of the mirror to embrace you

to understand what makes you come
touristing your way under the rainbow
into the old places where the wheat was sown

that fell from heaven
alphabets they planted in the ground
you reap in her and she reaps in you

the mirror healed and let you in
now there is no excuse for knowing
and nothing to be known

no excuse for saying anything
even if you do know a few words of Czech
stand quietly aside and let the tower fall

then speak if you have to and let it lift
and not a word yet about the flowers
the whole conspiracy you trust.

49.

Dried cartilage on the dock and far off
horizon line of dawn trawlers
sucking the sea up

indelicate digestion of the whalefish
mimicked by political history
in the convent of ill-transformed desires

where did I begin to go wrong in my analysis?
miss you terribly
history is everything you haven't thought of yet

that's how the stars start
udders of the cow Wasson's amanita
religion a safehouse for ecstasy

Veda the sun's confession to a passing cloud
of all She has not seen
the whole sky is repentance

the old bruise-purple fades from the hill
so the mind makes up a whole new day
carrying nothing over from the old

everything tries to go wrong
let it, liberty is always the other thing
when it forgets to look back at you from the mirror

then its work has really begun
paws remembering brain forgetting
nothing but the names of things.

You can't do it without numbers
all my life I've tried
but you can get there, at least arrive

footprint on naked sand and all
strange animals everywhere
naming you in their own way

mosquitoes will tattoo you
tonight on the new teak deck
and the moon try later to liquidate your brain

werewolf et cetera sleep inside my skin
come aboard the foundering space probe
that can't tell Nantucket from Aldebaran

there is a story here
if you'd just stop listening
stories only tell themselves to the reluctant

otherwise a story will die into
some other thing you've heard
where is nothing but sand in the wind.

50.

Ice-axe in a sort of Frenchman's hand
the weight of pilgrimage
stop listening or I'll never get done

sanguinaria still blooms white though Jackson's dead
today fell out of the mirror
strawberry spilled from the sultan's breakfast

my beliefs make me ridiculous
but ate it anyhow
and in the zenana girlful tittering.

51.

recursive moon our challenger
with saber nightly or this night scimitar
opening old wounds to vie with me

you show all your bruises, moon, and I hide mine
amazing what it means to be English
dryness of the heart dew on steering wheel

you hear the sea from anywhere you are
the seagull union still on strike
slippery elm for breakfast tea

there'll be a hunter here by noon
and then we hide our seaglass jewelry,
dream-soaked Pentagon

it all only seems to be rational
reason is just the color of the drapes that hide the mirror
and even money is a fitful dream

hard sun harries now
shut eyes to silence her
she has her interminable ways

every melody breaks at last
and then some sort of star falls
out of the tricky harmony

and landing among us incandescent
burns tiny holes in civil carpets,
music hurries always to an execution

52.

Then the sea was gone.
The hollow left behind it
filled up with sour gratitude

that it was done
and had to find something else
to talk about

the softness of hair
or how the stars secretly arrayed themselves
in Punic alphabets to spell a name

the propositional
is sentimental
whereas the refusal

to commit even a single sentence
sings, all the persons
in the dream are the dreamer

all persons in the world are
glittery facets, selves of the perceiver
no? No, the afternoon is different from the night

there are actual essences
sublations of negation into a desperate
playhouse of provisional identity

different children all
trying to pin the tail on the same donkey
while Jesus wept

so you admitted there is same
and he admits the differences
purple Vespas linguiça fat

cooling on a windowsill in France
things get around, Mascagni
merguèze, Transcendentalism

you name it, I just did
but what is our motivation in this scene
Byron baffled

most women and some boys
not enough of an answer
a bone hurt somewhere

an audience can always tell
can hear such pain
even from up there in the paradise

from which they barely see the diva's eyes
all they ever get is the color of things
disguised as tunes hidden in their ears

an audience can always hear the bone
creak of pain or grease of pleasure
surfing through the marrow

the long sad ache, no winged words
can lift his porky body off the stage
one millimeter into the applauding air

ramshackle rapture of the moment mind
crushed under this weird cargo
the images that they carry home

no room in their heads for the real
bank accounts and mortgages
through which they jostle in the street

a sneering moon over entertainment
when it's over, art is poison,
dawn's so grand because it's empty

means change can happen
otherwise it's some old play we're in
unless the Empty is.

53.

But if you burn a log a wolf has pissed on
in deep winter but it's summer now
some strange night cold sugars of his appetites

will dance in smoke above the franklin stove
filling the parlor with outrageous schemes
lust and bite and midnight chase

close that old book
old wolf is trotting still
no need for memory

forget the meat you bit or bite
don't let melody resolve
so quick inside the harmony your head

the malady of intercourse
there are sentence patterns here
you have to learn from listening

the opal sky gives way to grey and then to pearl
a little rain a little wind and thou
asleep beside me be wilderness enow

I wolf my way through the light
guided by cloud contours
brisk north wind shoves the sky out to sea

secateurs and flowers
only voices here no people
bodies come later

after the linguistic conventions are established
it's time for meat
and Entities come down to the surface of earth

to take up residence in the pronouns
to inhabit the language they had to make
flesho-mechanical bodies to manifest and control

the organs of articulation needed to speak
then ears to hear then hands to cover them
when the information grows too thick

and the Entity yearned for opalescent repose
east of the sea
where the strayed voluptuary tries to think of something else

only the images count
ignore the propositions
they're just armatures

to wind our bright things on
that teach us how to be and touch and to mean,
only the images

the story's for the sake
only of the instruments deployed
the scythe and the haystack, lipstick in the canoe.

I saw you part your lips last night
standing beside the bed I got in first
for a change you were putting lip balm on

standing there in your blue peignoir
and this is heaven I understood,
Eden was an accidental suburb of this moment

a cluttered Levittown of heaven,
heaven that is here now, thingly and will-free,
apocalypse of This.

54.

Morganatic marriage of moon and earth
all dance and no romance
the Polish army fleeing through the trees

and submarines, think about submarines
to live in metal underneath the sea
lilacs rotting on a spring hillside

Canada an ear against the wall
paper cup a blind man holds
he stomps through subway cars

smells bad he's not blind
he has no eyes he has leprosy
he stands in front of you and stamps his cane

right between your feet, give him a quarter
the sound of silver will cure the smell of skin
then his body totters down the train

but his image stays in your mind
forever those glaucous ruined eyes
all the dialects of blindness

his presence stinks all over you
but a mind inside as pure as mine
you think but how to reach it

a man like him has no inside you think and close your eyes.

55.

Mairead would be her Irish name
of pearl, *my read* it looked like
and I am her book

one of them, big for my age
caught in the reeds a while
then unfound, I found

myself I think while brother
Moses in the floating bassinette beside me
was hoisted by princesses

I endured in my floating condition
until language caught me mid-babble
and I spoke, god knows what I said

but it was enough to find me
later on a dry island
waiting for the weatherman to beg him for my life

my voice had not lost him in the woods
because a tree is a certainty
lifted by the angel air

the dawn wind dies down
as if the fierce sun slew it
shadows talking the waves still big

mottling sheen quick they pass through
mother of me the flame comes back
his eyes too close to every,

remembers the electric blue of her peignoir
first color he knew had a special name
a name drawn out of likeness or allegiance

kelly green and dyer's indigo
gold rings of women passing in the sun
they were his mothers too

enough of him the words
discuss, among themselves about themselves
like fetuses, global talkshow from the womb

until each word gets born
and born again in sad blue sentences
nobody really understands,

what have words got to do with bodies?
he paused and listened for a change
hoping there really was an answer

but just heard more whispering through dark rooms
hallway coming closer rustling
Ruskin fear the skin that touched so many

would touch me, fear the sea,
is that some kind of answer even
he should have been a rabbi

long walk in St. Albans Sunday
scuffling through prolific maple leaves
fallen scarlet and desperate and gamboge

so grab the memory by the middle
and deny it, Peter's third cockcrow
is always for you,

deny you ever knew these streets
faux-log gas fireplace Sunday night chop suey
deny while there's still time

to fill your head with other people's memories
sanitary and weird and good for you a little
nothing ever happened, believe it,

you're still floating in the reeds, right?
slim ankled princesses and priestesses
are all you ever see of human life

you can't tell the Civil War from the burning
tip of your father's cigar
yes you had a father a Pontiac a priest

put salt on your tongue
the lilacs flowered every April and the pussy willows
nuzzled your nose

nothing was lacking ever
just don't remember it
out loud, let it do its work inside

like a candle cheering up an empty room
iam satis and so on mind meadows
swollen and soaked with rain

remembering is rain.
Waterspout. Smell of turpentine.
Tristi fummo depressed we were

in the sweet fresh air *nel aer dolce*
all around us. Refresh us, terebinth,
Eve is painting her Tarot cards again

it will be years before she's done
that's what really goes on in Eden
her big panels, each one a Golden Section,

one by one till all are done,
the seventy-six *distinctions*,
every one of them a world

and each world segueing into all the others
no wonder she's at it all day long
and one of her cards is our own world,

The Three of Coins I think
shows God creating this world and putting
Eve and Adam in it, a workless garden

from which they fled and all this followed—
there's just this one card though
love and high magic means turning all the others

becoming those worlds too
hurry out of this, out of all the sentences proposed,
the so-called gardens,

each new card shows the way away
as one by one she paints them and displays
and though we're locked in our poor old Trey of Diamonds,
    say,

we still can see hers, all the rest she's painted
(but she's not done) stretching out before us
where we stretch our eyes ahead to analyze

at moonless midnight intercepts
the southern islands of the Milky Way
chill discomfort a million other worlds

you'll get around to living in
just close your eyes.
But you were sad, *tristi*, weren't you

in the glad air that surrounds our curious planet
glum and hopeless of setting hands
on the milksoft skin of God

so catching even one glimpse of the actual
you read the papers and got depressed
Lancelot jangled past, Guinevere sidled by

with a flurry of frangipani, you tasted ginger
and still were sad
depression is an addiction, no,

a substanceless dependency
"after being drawn from the object   *(K. Abraham)*
the libidinal investment returns to the ego"

stuck in the mud
fearful to reach out
and hating those who can

years after years remain newborn
attending the seducer's hand
that never comes.

Being cheated is a kind of answer
Onan at the blackjack table
scattering white chips across the board.

56.

Forget the target
the *arrow itself*
is the instruction

make it go faster
by looking at it hard
we are committed here to do and not to be

being comes later
in what you call heaven
and I call now

she said, a smudge
of Prussian blue
longside her cute nose

we sunset from the garden
east into evidence
to know the world

reverse the flow
he cried and leapt
from the cruel ramparts of Albi

into the confusion of history
we'll never know anything for sure
only what we make up is certain

and even then who can be sure
of all the famous assassinations in the heart
or whose shadow holds the knife whose shadow falls?

as a farmer looks out at the first light
and does not know if that red gleam
means storm he fears and farewell wheat or

it's just an ordinary dawn releasing
all the quiet blood the night consumed
who knows where colors come from anyhow

sécheresse du cœur he blamed me for
as I folded all my own shadows under my cloak
and hid in the crowded subway

where workmen used to whistle at that hour
but nobody whistles anymore in public
decline of self made music music lost its lips.

57.

understand not so solemn
Hegel it's hard
think my think before me

fiori or am I even yet
birth of the belated
storm coast you never hear

what happened to the real
unappeared
your face among philosophers

what word is this
what catamaran leaping through the Cut
a girl made of glass

pheromones of mind are too
they can abstain across a room
in musicless novitiate

what are you saying saying
that sophophily knows it doesn't know
and wants to, does not content

itself with analysis of if-norance?
is it new religion
more like a cake with nuts in it

hazel for wisdom
and Deborah endures lewd dreams
beneath her palm tree

and Moses's long lost brother me
eats Chinese apples,
the whole Bible story just one Tarot card if that.

58.

Missing is a devious art
and needs its Aeschylus
whose poetry would be a vast forgetting

one morning she was gone
and all the rest was hurting
I suppose we would call that thinking

and in disorder something more
an urgent Christian 'burn
only in your heart, leave

the stake to those who believe in the state,
banish martyrdom,
jihad is a massacre within'

as if there were a way to do it
overtake the wind and freeze the rainbow
hold everything in mind

keep balance, *halte Maaß*
said Dürer, keep the measure,
understand divine proportion in your hand

then change my name
I never liked me anyhow
thirty years gone but it remembers

purr of the car's engine
idling, but who was the woman
and the river and who is the moon?

59.

We change the lines but it cannot change,
starbeam trapped forever in our amber
★ put there as an easy sign

so the knowers know and the doers forget
and both be darkened by a random thought
the same pretty little cloud, *nuvoletta,*

star and heart must rhyme in some language
the mark on the wall that means
movement in your soft mouth

a sound in the cave—like an engine idling—
apposition they taught: to set
two or more words in balance

so each casts its glow and shadow on the other
arid though the space around the signs but not between,
the between of anything is the loveliest tune.

60.

No action in the Achaean fleet assembled
even killing has to wait for night
uneasy shepherds grumbling at their sheep

this is no place for an animal
a man with eyes
something is about to begin to begin

arms spread to catch
a living noise from the sky
old women wore veils when I grew up

matrons' eyes behind violet organdy
gauzy with little flecks of flowers
a line looped round the light

always had to coat their presences
or else they'd overwhelm us
too much evidence, too many islands

sometimes things are done and never know it
a court hand engrossing a charter
all good comes from the Queen

to her I recommend this rubble
comely pebbles on a midnight ocean
lit only by the intelligence

the dark pain that can't help seeing—
and it is only that special pain that *sees*
only the pain that understands the door

and the little boy who watched the fire exit
all through the movie and understood
that led to the real mystery

the thing outside the theater
on the other side of all this art
but you could only get there through this confusion

there, waiting for him out there,
a thing in a world of things
a thing is patient,

often they told him about heaven
he guessed it was a place
where understanding was,

they knew the answers and they told you
and you saw the back side of the moon.
But what if the dead are as dull as the living

what if nobody knows?
What if there's nothing really there
and you have to make it up new every time

or bring it with you
knowledge squeezed through confusion
like a child being born into this world

and there it would be in the other
a gasping knowledge full of pain and relief
licked into shape by a weird (that is, fated) geology

where stones are soft again
and cool fire plays around your hips
and it isn't about knowing at all it's about saying

a poem is a ouija board without the wood
it shows you where you want to go
the sea is no color but the sky

try it drink it all down
and see what colors are left
words are always looking for silence

a text always in love with the end of itself
gnomic palaver, meat on your plate
then forget theory, Nietzsche is just mustard now

changes the taste of what you think
just enough to make you think he thought it
the Crucified, the one with powerful ideas

until he sang, music
is no way to please the Muses
or only one way and watch the waiter move

and the hostess perched behind the reservation book
and TV crews devouring this same stew
we thought was our food our life our destiny

we have no destiny
we only have what we found in a book
the taste in someone else's mouth

when we say I love you and they say nothing
and what is there for music to say
the philosopher collapsed in the street

the philosopher endured a restriction in discourse
we do not know the words he said in that condition
sun and moon go hide and seek

you grow up part of a time machine
we're at the stage where only kindness helps
publish it not in the streets of Askelon

no one listens to the silence in the heart
whose sound is it one thing can save us
us us always you're talking talking

there is no us, that's the problem
if there were us we would be living at this hour
not this rain of flies on Pershing Square.

61.

Turn into that which you desire
reinstate the heart of the other
in the heart of the self

and a gull has pointed wings
that go in two directions he is not going
we are in the country where things turn into themselves

no syntax left, nothing to hide,
a growl of hunger deep in the cave of same
where we wait our turn in the sun glare

the names we give our obsessions
go there and buy something
buy something that knows you

that knows your secret name
buy a day-old rose from country gardens
a tune I guess you've heard before

or always knew but you
are on the other side of music—
the devil licked it with your tongue

skin-tight clothing of the rock
loose lubricity of the sea's peignoir
green as amber why did you say that

how do you let yourself be so wrong
because a breeze speaks me
an air inside the understanding

like a cardinal of the church
or a martyr burning
still mindful into the exhausted air

that's what he meant by turning
something into what it is
already from the beginning sea without land amen.

62.

Daodejing Thomas Meyer made me
bristling with silences
wind solves fire fire solves rock

and so it flows, the old man asleep for once
the ox trudges on
made in China like the mulberry

paper the stone jar
the jade man the size of a man
nothing on earth shyer than a word

63.

Do you belong here
(bird in sky provisional
arrangement, stone on stone)

do shadows all around the room
look like yours
cast by the opacities of your (and only your)

house? that means your body
that means what it sees and feels
what casts a shadow, yours?

the snake on the lawn is yours
the white iris by the porch, yours,
too many things belong to you

and where do you belong?

64.

woodcock willet birds of island
kingbird catbird bobolink
blackbird grackle robin dove

and far out the western cliffs one day two crows
not otherwise known here
among all the swallows and seagulls and terns

waiting personages barges boats
miracle cures for yesterday
hazy breezy grommet

angry tern hover over
Holy Ghost white dove once
on the ceiling of the old church in Morzine

I read his delicate beak.

65.

delicate work of being somebody else
anatomy of a scream
I parse

phantom agony you remember sober
carrying bottles
filled with your own fake wine up the elevator

to a floor you never reached before
I try to write this down with a gold pen
that glisters iridescent in morning sun

more than I know how to make words do
except by what they're pointing to
seraph glistering slippery traces of you.

66.

Being on the way to
the other side of somewhere
is being home

the mountains of yesterday
are full of thin sheep
the oracle said

full of rain mist moving
shaping new language for the eyes
speak the mist deeper

into the almost opaque colors of a word
there is no need to speak
philologist of necessity

an artisan of the unknown must break stone.

67.

Evander was king up that elmy river
but we need to fight the Calico Wars again
fight the landlords—no man pay no rent—

occupancy is possession—
burn all the records
come home from Baghdad and do that now,

the thrust of education
is to keep the poor in their place
and balance cheap labor with passionate consumers

history maximizes profit for the few
we know all this why say it again
because I keep forgetting

genuflecting in philanthropized museums
gentrification of the neighbor mind
until the young bride's ring

slips off Mélisande's finger
and farewell wishing well
no more shanachie or wedding bells

the multitudinous waves of greed
— pretty enough as they break up on our shore —
aesthetics is the knack of making do

with the terror of the situation
teaching the poor to feed on pure perception
the blind man tasting sugar with his hands.

68.

Religion is getting things without having them
just lift the wooden latch on the flimsy paper door
and all the world's your dancing floor

we've had our little squall of lucidity
cloud full of propositions
just like you, resemblance is bad for the soul,

the contradictions, bella, keep us going,
and drunkenness and all the arguments
spun out from the chancelleries of prose

be young with me at last
I never was the thing you am
but always other, your oldest child

just be young with me in magic doubt
touching for good luck
the witchcraft trees of every passing woods

and genuflect before the moment only
only the instant is beautiful
the light that shows through

between the seams and fissures of the actual
how far I am from knowing who
is all you need to know

doing something to the flow of time
loosening something tightening something
maybe the same thing letting something go

concelebrate with dragons
tone roads isomorphic tyrannies impose
you get the feeling you're not supposed to feel

the trains walk on time
but let me go on sleeping
do they have lightning on the moon

can I get a room with just one candle
and no shadows, a bathroom with no mirror,
a morning with no check-out time

and a peephole in the door to know who passes
and another in the wall so they can look at me
that I might know myself in their admiration

look at me so that I live
I am the occupant of the room
and have a clock of my own

listen you can hear the stationmaster's lament
a train that takes them all to prison
and never do what your heart tells you to

because the true heart knows no doing
just sit there listening till everything is done
answer the phone before it rings.

69.

As a start a stare
at a star
but where is the body

you stand in
the shoulder you hurt
hoisting something too big for your age

a box
to put books in
where it all began

the transgressions
you understand it now
the wrong things you always did

looking up at stars down at book
but where was the hither prospect
the right before your nose

the world between?
o shy is the shape
of the other in the self

shimmer of silence shy in you
when the other speaks
and shy too, inky dark,

it is dark between the ears
and you were raised to love martyrs
the self-slain altar-bound heroes

lions ate them and fire burned
but better a live thinking you think
than a dead believer

enough for you nowadays
the purple heather up lookout hill—
is that maturity or corruption

maybe you'll never know
at least the star stares back
the way an island off the coast

is yours for the looking
shifting in and out of fog and the flowers
in the graveyard, who looks at them,

face me when I'm speaking
answer the nice flowers
silk ones the lady

she wears them on her hat
she wears a little veil
she sits on a throne

the throne is made of her,
the veil is made of flowers
to hide her quiet eyes

as if whatever I must speak
she needs but does not desire—
need without desire I have fled all my life

when I have done with silence.

70.

Tree in the window of the particular
what kind? sycamore she thought
its white bark blamed with ivy

broken syntax trying to tell you
an orchestra is always ending something
you leap onto the bare stage

and everyone can see you but me
because I was born blind in a bible
only words fit my teeth

nothing to see
but the dissolving alphabet
whose residue is everything I touch.

71.

Pay-pal Satan a laptop a laptop!
eye-beams still entangled
structural element all the age of Huizinga

the unpronounceable wisdom
lila not *laila* play
might save us, not night serve us,

awkward customers
desire desired, dared
crow call in the common market

myspace nullspace now
your pronouns will be the death of you
not by vocabulary was Rubicon

the quartan ague hath harrowed me
culex or anopheles Assam
a score of years blood varmint

invisible architecture of malaise
economist measuring the tide
in ownership or null

the true believer
sobbed with Comenius from thoughts of exile
Return, Return the voice repeated

until the other chambers of his brain
listened and told the heart
what it had not heard

you have to shout for the heart to hear
over the engines of its conscious will
—Go home—Where is home?

Right here right here inside
the eternal politics of personal identity
the only god whose name you know

the light thick as you are
intersection flooded thigh-deep
cloud shadows course the spontaneous lagoon.

72.

Thirty years been gospelling
Republic of the Common Shore
the unowned pronounless dimension

high tide and low tide
the real estate between
I suppose a child to walk there

now how to make this stretch of beach
its screech of tern and hush of surf
reach out and tinge the knowable

to drown world maps
under kelp and sea glass
emeralds for the common man

just bend down
and belong to what you find
you are mine then in that minute

catch a sparrow by its go
the fugitive habit
preaching over your shoulder

we go down into the salt meadow to make priests
out of girls and slingshot astronomers
knock the stars out one by one.

73.

Until your own stars light up the sky
only in perfect darkness Lancelot
can you see your way home

still a zany personal voice persists
until the last star goes out
afraid of wanting too much

afraid of not wanting you at all
mercy is a local star
cloud edged in porphyry and iris

the sunset on this river imported
from a larger sky and barely fitted
over the River that Flows Two Ways

baptize the child again and again
till you get the name right
silence of corn silence of dawn.

74.

In the market memory
(canon on flarf)
go back to bed still morning

we have business with noon
a knife and a bull
once you've turned you can't unturn

perversion is a grammar of its own
that understands and reassorts
fruits of the earth and sea

turning everything that should have form
the sky is window-shopping us
that's what flarf means

free language abandons standard function
and sneaks into your mind direct
without the "inconvenience of meaning"

natural noise ill-guided by our codes
gilded? gelded? both of these
nomina barbara without a hint of child

science has much to learn
from Dharma
nothing at all the other way round.

75.

Dear person the pursuit
changes names in the dream
the fox gives me three bites

one for history
one for God
one to learn her name

I choose and choose to say it
muted a little by my history
by the strange apocopations of the dream

soft cliffs of Norfolk near the Admiral Nelson
I knew I had come home
sitting naked in the dark to catch the air

window fan and its whir
Browne carried into his meditation
telling me nothing more

than Canaletto's light for daytime
de la Tour's light on skin at night
the cliffs crumble if you write in them

just like Oregon just like memory
a finger does it
let it be faster than love

and laster, Easter every Sunday
and very, let the farmer's market
fill up with she-goats, be my nomad

always come back to me
your special purgatory that
this body is, am,

will answer all your questions
it will pretend to be light
falling through the leaves or breaking

into curious shadows of leaves on your white wall
your sea wall
water flooding through your hands

like sea glass color of the eyes you see it with.

76.

the nomad always has another planet up his sleeve
bewildering autumn warblers
only the yellow ones get spotted but all of them sing

then rush to meet it in a book
where someone else's name for this experience
is sold to you and the bird is gone

how long is a line
from silence to silence the shortest word—
that is a line

word, what is a word
across a room the deepest touch
now you're being faintly fraudulent

romanticism is mechanical
when applied to people,
it is not a reaction to the industrial revolution

it *is* the industrial revolution,
privileging matter and methods of production
the divine artificer, Jacquard at his loom,

Shelley among thorns
how they make us feel,
sell your soul to the devil

doomed poet can't even break the light
has no shadow, can't cast a shape on matter—
because romanticism is all about production

about having some effect, about causing
perturbation in the system, nature and marriage,
about leaving a mark

because romanticism is Roman is Rome
is rule and sentimental grammar
and ego-worship, where Caesar's god

is Caesar's self
and god is anyone you pick to pay
your bloody bulls and barley to

or at midnight squealing pigs
to Hecate
pine cones on fire.

77.

There is a letter of the alphabet like a muddy road in
    Sweden
where Joseph Martin Kraus wept for the king his dead lover
there is a letter like sun rising through smog industrial haze

fold what you know as a self into a letter
and be this letter
so birds fly right through you

you have come near the nesting place
the sources of life
always in the rocks always edge of the sea

they dive all round you
they void their glad cloacas on your hat
if you're the kind of letter that has a hat,

write yourself a letter and send it to me
or leave it by the apple tree
the last one left at the construction site

yellow helmet hanging from the branch
leave it there or under midnight
give other loves a chance to find it

one letter fills up the whole page
and then I'll know you, have you,
I'll tell what I know to no one not even the tree,

nobody knows what the sea's saying either
because it speaks so beautifully
all form and no information.

78.

The woods green moveless sea
click of wood clirr of leaf
insects at their never-ending plainchant offices

no Palestrina to relieve the rise the flex the fall
of what is permanent
and yet it moves

but how do you know, he said,
what Homer's ocean sounded like to him
your Latin's rusty and your Greek's been repossessed

sometimes you hear what fleshy Virgil heard
sometimes you guess
sometimes you pick a letter and become it

like a girl in a casino tricked to choose a card
by some devious entertainer with more sleeves than arms
says here you are, the Three of Diamonds,

there is no alphabet in wood
in woods
I am alone

in the middle of the alphabet
I came to water
and there was her name beginning

the bitter sea and all its pearls
and the great tower she came from
to meet me there,

follow a line as long as it goes
till it leads to yourself
pick the right letter turn into a god

powerlessly beautiful
no romanticism here
here is yielding here is letting

here is language listening to itself and letting go
so you can have some too
if you don't become a letter the word will never speak

patch of sun on forest floor
the leaves make faces
a progression of identities procession carnival silence

the leaves are masks
all we know how to see are faces
so the leaves make faces at me

the belongers huddle beneath the shade
an austere text rustles
rebuking every image.

79.

Crawl out from under the skirts of the world
into the evidence
no more sentiment, material man,

specify the rigorous ardors of your music
the count the spell
backwards in your steps

to the organ tone that started this
16Hz below your ears
marble slabs the floor make shudder

understand what you can't hear
fear also is a vibration
something you can learn from, lean on

the Ascent (assent) to Parnassus
shy man's guide to the muses
his eyes on something else the music rises

and by the strangely tempered disposition of his tone
suddenly he's out—
you've heard it a thousand times

but you always climb back in
—you call that listening—
instead of traveling onward with the final tone

or *klang* as it recedes
orderly into the summoning distances
whose only property you can guess by reason

is silence
but it is so much more so that
the proper hearing of music is a one-way road

let it take you as far as you can hear
material man, then
travel with it and never look back

looking back means drowning in the tune
the Red Sea
looking back is remembering

into the unconditioned paradox
where music vanishes before you
a fox in sumac and you follow.

80.

I bought my soul from the devil.
Yes. What do you think he does
with all those souls he buys,

Faust and all the rest of them,
Hoffmann, Peter Schlemihl?
He sells them, and sells them dear,

if you spend your whole life working
—for God or me, makes no difference
just keep at it—

all your life and every day
you can buy this anguished tarnished soul
full of vile lusts and tedious appetites.

81.

clock in wood work
golden fear
touch me I am your last idea

it said in the leaf
from flarf a genesis
yet from tone row not

an infinity of tunes
but audible absence
of any you to hear.

82.

The king went sailing up the vein
and came into the wind where the lungs were
and there he was reborn not for the first time

insidious repetitions of desire
gold flake flee occasion
she showed herself willing to be mortal

more me! more me!
corner or kernel
angle of Galois' last night

dreamy discharge on the margin
of all he had no time left
to make literal

already the girl he died for
was running through the meadow
already in some other opera

pretending she rode a zebra in Zululand
pretending to be motionless in church
pretended to be sitting on her chair

and all the while the bullet silenced him
such a strange story! but my teacher
guided me away from the field of honor

saying There is no honor here
honor is only where the blood is springing
invisible meaningful alive in living being

and then my teacher set his palm over my eyes
and led me through what felt like caves of ice
though my eyes were heavy carrying what they'd seen

dying mathematician grieving woman trilling through
     the woods
keening banshee so in my heart
some woman always is lamenting

but I never told my teacher that
for fear he would silence her
then where would I be, unguided by grief?

83.

Carve silence, churl, carve
absence into aroma
you don't miss their faces you miss their sheen

ælfscin or aura, the light around one
that makes her who or him she is,
elf-shine the preter-human shown,

faërie folk are what we must become,
elves are not some belated ancient lingerers
they are our *future selves*

keen wise dangerous and rife with pleasures
we catch a glimpse of them sometimes
when the moon or noon be right

and the shadow falls
they are we will be
and till then be quiet, read your tree.

84.

What Nietzsche forgot to tell us
we dream the gods
but the gods when they doze dream numbers

and leave their scary measures as the world,
caliper music Fibonacci fractals
fiddling with the coasts of every where

the clutter of contradictory proportions
halte Maaß he cried and drew a pensive woman
with her soft bottom pressed on a chiseled rock

this is Melancholia this is thoughtfulness.

85.

This is the ailment of the thoughtful,
the need to touch and not desire
the energy of abstinence

by which a formal world is shaped
by silence alone the body's made
red clay on your soft white soul

you showed your palms
to read the lines
here is commitment

here is the zoo you saw sleek seals in
here is the zebra you rode naked on a dare
here are the children you will not have

here is your mother nodding by the fire
here is your final journey by water
and here is Jerusalem the faithful city

you'll go there in language
one night in the desert you will crouch down
here is the moon, here is you beneath it.

86.

Zebra. Part of, sea. With stripes
a bass, a rock pointing into the wind.
Always. Straits of some word you can read.

Tread. Your name. The will.
A hoof, a hard place in the sky,
buy wounds, north wind, lethe,

remember lethe, cross, spear, hammer,
zebra, ankle, past of the sea
retold to children, their skin

purest ivory from tusk of slain beast
narwhal. walrus. zebra, your name
riding on another's, crown, a bead of spit

pearl on your lip, revenge, for what
pocket calculator hidden in whose clothes
determines measure? hold mass, hold me

bridge, wine, rock, fish, cloud,
capax, neuter, nimble, rim,
prod, press, hold, forget, dwell.

Dwale, dwindle, then wake up
lady in waiting, cork, spill, taper,
gizmo, little flame, name,

noonless name, agglutinative, frost,
cat ice, dowel, rosary, semaphore,
meat rack, woman at loom, leaf,

laugh, gull, trajectory, channel,
mirror, corridor, oration, barley,
shadow, shelter, moorland, zebra.

87.

A kind of scar left on time
like the sabbath,
a ripple in feeling

sleep with her,
go back to the original
agreement, garden,

colonial remorse,
take your coastlines with you
like a bundle of wet clothes,

be gone into beauty,
a breast at the window
the city a stranger to this night

reflection of setting sun that color
only city windows show, gold-red over Rego Park
abominable exaltation of sheer light,

end of the family, end of Mao,
learned men at public villainy
all that passes and this light stays

because somebody built a wall
and put a window in it
someone set a sun in the sky and left it to fall

tangled like Courbet, with no covers,
treadmill, lovers, long curving corridors
seafoam on my sand I lick the rock

in love with where it's been
and it can't tell, what we love best
are our guesses, the grove of hope

through which some times some things come
quietly to meet us and we know
we were right, and right for once is right forever.

What we love best is what we think,
our take on everything that passes
and the few things that try to stay,

your name, your keys on the table
she found when you lost them,
the paper clip, blatant amaryllis of Christ's wounds.

88.

People who lose the debate are called heretics
people who win the debate are called the police
they play this game mostly in the countryside

gods seem touchier under elms
or down among the pagan alders
godlings sulk until in turn you touch

they love us best when we desire,
don't even have to desire them,
he said, even me will serve

o love he cried
o where the subject is lost in the object
o the sublation of our reluctancy

into plain passion
we are not sure of our desire we insist on it
love o great testing ground of want

o love is always changing the subject
kissing my cheek twenty years later and saying *I ... you*
clearly in my ears so that it stays there

like the feel of a hip where my hand rests
he said when there was breathed into me
that numberless information I require

relays opening and closing
old-fashioned dream machine
a hapteme stimulates my fingertip

this is what the ancients called *creatio mundi*
not a thing that dares to happen only once
the cosmogonic time is every moment

the primal scene writhes in front of you
whenever you open your pretty eyes
this game all full of goneness.

89.

slowly the gods come back
that is the news
today, their names come first

bandied about by analysts and universities
then their great long bodies come
dawn-skinned, difficult to grasp

but palpable the way you are
when a breeze knows the back of your neck
you know they're here the way you know music

imagine the taste of a rose in a dead man's mouth
or shadow in a rabbit's fur
the gods were like that

taste of sugar in a mute man's mouth
but now they're coming back
they are on all sides now, our side,

Holy Scamander! they're with us in our fight
some say the Wickings brought them here
or merchant Greenlanders far as New York Narrows

say anything that comes into their why-not heads
and I am some of some of them too
I have as much right to be wrong as anybody

so when I pour out milk and wine to you
as mete libation to your sacral presences
I will be wrong today and right tomorrow

the gods are always
but are not always here
then they are, hear them hearkening to us,

smoking is evil because it's incense
you offer to yourself and not to them
a smoking priest is a heinous thing

unless he's in their possession, *loa,* and they in him
take pleasure in his indulgence,
the gods are pleasure, are only pleasure,

the god rules the *strong man* and he needs his cigar
but that's Brazil and sugarland and here we are
single in eternity

obsessed with the feel of things
rain rapture voice on telephone even
thrilling murk of human notice

blame me, you. He is obsessed with you.
You are his theology and arithmetic
his history book and geology,

such power you innocently ignorantly wield
just by being and being other. Over there,
lucid, out of self's reach, sky blue, you.

90.

but never enough
like a wanton with her pricey tail
all over the provisional café

you call it dancing
I call it god coming into focus at last
Lorca's *duende* comes home now

men fall in love with skin
our largest organ, spreadsheet of the soul,
pheromones and highway maps

you go to bed with a body but you marry skin
because there are so few
whose pale maps can match your terrain

these are your wife.
Permanent inexorable true as an island
I know the boat that goes there

they caught an eel but let it go
it led them from creek to creek across wet grass
rain helps them trust the beast

helps them move, the journey is material,
they follow the easiest lines
in this world easy is hard enough

sore bones and barriers
Melchizedek the rightwise king
who has no name but what he does

for *do* read *who*, for *yes*
read *some*, for *no* read *me*
open-armed waiting for your wings

I am obsessed with pure arrival
he said, this weakens me
in my daily conflict with the real, i.e.,

the already arrived, yesterday's paper,
owl feather on the lawn
from a war in heaven

I said nothing, there was no image
except the barred feather pale and dusty brown
and wonder where the owl went

out the actual back yard into the imaginal
a pearly house where such birds soar
even he, giving pleasure to the sultan with their calls

for the owl's cry is tentative caress
a whisper in your canal, a truth
perched on the pinna of your ear it seems

so close her declarations are
the oracles speak one line at a time
the whole line makes a single word

one word itself is a whole religion,
no I answered, here there is no *is*,
we have sailed at last beyond the proposition

touch me it said and someone did
here all the stories end
after seven hundred years of snowy searching

bruised by implication
the book falls silent
life itself is an encryption—

the history of literature tries to conceal
how each age hides this secret:
writing is always to someone

how else could the breath rise to speak
and Virgil wept
remembering the little boy where Palinurus lay

a shepherd boy for whose unbidden sake
he learned the names of sheep and wrote them all down
in lucid meter, calmly, his eyes full of tears,

tears the Tuscan wept for him later
letting them course out,
river of eternal misunderstanding,

a little boy looking at the sea
and who *was* this Achilles
Homer loved so much in his dark?

91.

A wife is a fruit in somebody's hand
a large ancient man falls in love
to use the language of the gutter

but gods in love with his javelin
his diamond-studded belt his orisons
his love songs his amazing self-deceptions

slew Orion into a thing in the winter sky
the gods made him a constellation: this means
they took him away, they hid him living

among the stars, always near us, breathing,
the gods are so good at hiding, hid him in plain sight
his gleaming eyes above us all winter long

they hid him deep inside our explanations
we lost the story and barely look at the stars
so the man, little more than a boy, really, just married,
    is gone

hunting heaven with the ruby tip of his spear
harrying you too night by night
as you toss and turn in hot explaining,

but who are these gods
these beings who live only in explanations
and maybe in the thunder round my house

woke me at first light
but who's me
the rain that tricks the flowers into thinking,

practice idle flower
every island has its Ariel
the squeeze of weather

commercial transaction poetry
keeps the meter hold
trade value of each expression as

cod, cod cheeks, hake,
corned hake, flounder, fluke,
those are commodities are foods

words are the culls of the system
the one-armed the unsellable
we give away, here and there

a word with two claws gets through the screen
and comes to you, say by cell phone,
and tells the bareback truth just once

until the halfling words all round devour it
when it is eaten up and gone
it is a myth again

safe in the Milky Way inside you
the lights by which you journey inward
you and I, it really is about us after all,

the Town Explainer is part of the town
the further language gets from conversation
it darkens in Narcissus's mirror

sermons are a natural part of talk
(*sermo* = conversation)
that's why I sing you what I want for lunch.

92.

All sounds are phantoms do you know that
I stood and thought about it like a trumpet sounding
I did not understand it very long

a sound he said is just a revenant
a brief scar of something that happened to the air
sounds are ghosts that come to haunt you

hang out for years and fears in
the dank cathedral of your recollections
melody by melody until

you can hear no more, ghosts
of someone's mouth and ghosts of hammer blows
no difference in the rain

what must I do with this information
take it to the rose
the primitive the one by sea cliffs springing

amidst all the inversions of your attention
sea-glass lawnmower sacred fraction
mosaic doubts, cruciform bryophytes

and whisper this: all sounds
are this sound, this kiss
is every kiss, there is no difference

there is no special mouth.
Just staircase and parking lot forever
cars bake in sun inside the dew-soaked rose

or is it one more time your moist breath
condenses on the cooler petal
sunshine and attitude, things still left to buy

drugs to silence the distances
just like the time before and still it hurts
just like now but actually it's gone?

93.

What's so real about reality?
Cordovan shoe polish celery seed
slate anecdote bay tree thickets

wings, tines, tombs, tell me wax
gouge a music from conversation
with a screwdriver slept on the stairs

soft as a washcloth her self in bed
no names almost sober especially
soaked grass but a view of the window

dark bed and the emperor passes outside
and who lies there dying or writhing
or is it just settling a quilt around themselves

alarming tendencies of objects (I-less things)
to act like subjects (I have seen the emperor!)
sinister espresso device, a pillow with ideas

(such a huge horse!) not so simple, anglo,
not so white and smirk the end of history,
things are the stars by which we move,

floundering vapors in love with solidity
but all we do is buy and sell
never taking deep upon ourselves

the changeless suchness of the actual.
But isn't this just *Becoming?*
Just then the toaster sang

and the mail fell out of the ceiling
and the house was a dream again,
all road and no go.

94.

Now it is sunny and the dream must die.
Never tell and always told.
A brick for breakfast with a letter baked in it

resistance an affection of the wrist
stolen vocabulary unmined
bookless readers itchy tongues

do not frustráte me o my darling
let the sad tune have just once a happy ending
why should it when nothing does?

cut the opera before the death scene
let the curtain down while they still sing
and let the audience stroll fantasizing home

music knows no longitude
Ein Lied geht um die Welt they sang
just before the U-boats did

we call this the dead man window
music's boring unless you listen,
hearing it just kills you.

95.

Unlicked postage stamp how long till we kiss
turn on the spine the old brain needs caress
kundalini on the prowl her tongue flickers

waves the mint away and brings you in her mouth
to kiss and taste and eat a serious quince
from the Tree of Thee, knowing well and ill

this picture is the only one we know
girl instructed by the serpent's mouth,
the tree, the man astonished at this conversation

which is a turning, things turn into one another
as Dante shows the snake and thief inturning
and we amazed at his descriptive skill

perceive—or guess—what he's too busy to—
that transmutation is the essence of our liberty
that we can slough our properties and take

others on and then the same again
timelessly varying till we get it right
no snake no thief no theology

the starward shift instead
come out of the desert, Miriam,
you have been too many men already

let her nude breakfast bring
let her palm sing
let henna tell her hair

the stars are everywhere around us
not just up there
and every line a maxim for my mother

an honest answer (Dora to Freud)
is always physical
how could we trust a word to speak

it's what does the talking tells
hence the lyre-horns of the alpha ox
we string and strum

coaxing vowels out of matter, see
or whistle in the reeds at midnight
till even I am born.

96.

And Eve took it from the serpent's mouth
the Latin says so and the picture proves it
and ate it and Adam looked on greedily aside

until she gave him too
ab ore serpentis
where had it come from

how did the snake come by it?
Got it from Gilgamesh
who left it by the lakeside the riverside

when he was weary and sweaty
and stepped down to bathe
and the serpent stole it

says the story but I think
it had always belonged to him,
to her, a fruit-like jewel that was her own

and this in Edenic generosity
she writhed up the tree to give to Eve,
but what was that fruit, or flower—

it may have been a fleshy flower
old-men-are-young-again or the one called Live Forever
or the leafless blossom of the lone paulownia

that stands up in the graveyard
ombudsman for the island's dead
foretelling nothing.

A fruit with no promises,
a taste with no consequences
just the understanding ego

with something sudden, sweet in its mouth.

97.

imperfectly like a root
but truthfully like a wasp nest
its vague symmetry

joyfully like a fingernail
blue with dirt
the gardener's moon

but givingly also bent low with deciding
from a riot of immigrants
choose one accurate wife.

98.

You feel about god the way men
feel about their fathers
fondly over their shoulders fare thee well

the lover comes to the beloved
with no rose but hands
and this null rose

doesn't have to know so much
patriot of silence
moving hollow-fisted among crowds

showing the sign of your closed lips.

98.

Canticle of Adam

The bird brought it
you called it afternoon
I cupped it in my mouth

the birds were different then
I want to be empty
the way your mouth was

I had to take it in
to swallow everything
what food can empty me

people were different then
they said anything
came into their heads

it didn't have to mean
the same thing every time
things were different then

lay light on my hand
say soft beneath you
you liked the taste

the word liked me.

100.

But what do you do after understanding?
silence in one heals thousands
Seraphim of Sarov said

little cabin in the snowy woods
a cheesy poem rules the empire
a star of need you put it there

the sky's only ten miles away
easy enough to put a new star there
our government of trolls will never notice

public policy a naked lunatic
screaming in the street
don't go there I see the yellow

wolf eyes of your argument
better be silent better be Sarovsky
and the silent throng of pilgrims

watching the snow flakes settle
and blessing every one, *tardif*,
with equal slowness falls.

101.

Solue, coagula

stalwart if swarthy a script
fallen from the Producer's hand
the cinema is a *dissolving* art

poetry a *concretizing* one—
both are needed for your alchemy.
We visit the dump, we camp

on the slope of the grassy landfill hump
from which here and there vents
from underground burn blue with methane

corpse gases, bale fire.
It is as much like a Ganges ghat
as we can find near home or tolerate

the blue demonic glimmer I love well
the smell the sense of being on an earth
unsteady, uneasy in its gut,

as the minor asteroids hurry towards
their long delayed conversations
with us o my god it really could be

dead land with no corpses
just the quiet blue flame like little neighbor stars
and down below us corruption and new forms

res nova 'new thing' meant rebellion in old Rome
a bad thing to be new
or blue, or rhyme with anything, even you

Claudia, elegant trollop, handmaiden
of a timeless word you make him speak
timid rebel with his head on fire

with the taste of you all thyme and wine
can you distinguish your beauty in all his many
songs shaped exactly like your ear?

102.

Ocean understanding
the child possesses everything he can think
she thinks and the old man

in the Hampstead garden
among his costly flowers saw
no reason to change her mind

the ocean thinks in us.
In some books he had read
the White People actually come

down from the moors or the moon or the suburban line
to console with their immense difference,
the *transparent language* they whisper to the child

so he looks at Freud with sympathy
he knew (he was sure) he knew
but only hinted in his exciting though rather turgid books

he knew the child knows *everything* and chooses
the systematic metaphors by which to live
this whole new life to come, the untellable story

Freud yearned with all his lust to hear
from sumptuous analysands upon his divan,
not the supine babble of their conscious games

he had to listen so hard to penetrate—
and woman after woman he listened to
to hear the real story beneath the told, and sometimes did,

it's all about listening, that much he knew
and said and taught, but his "talking cure"
cured not the one who spoke but the one who listened.

103.

Pelasgic Freud meant, the ocean feeling
illimitable appetite to apprehend
in the new mind knowing

interpenetrates and impregnates
the object of its scrutiny
without actually having it, Eden of recency,

language comes later, when a child
starts forgetting the First Language,
the immediate answering of first knowing,

and learns human language out of courtesy
to share with others a little bit of what the child
knows so well but why did the others forget?

I know this. I was a child, knew the pain
of trying to share, break what I knew
into pieces small enough to say

to get the words right
and they never were, hardly
ever are, even now

o god the things we clearly dearly know
and never tell, every single one of us
a Dante in the dark

hence all the fuss of listening
hard, to hear the story
behind what is told, outrageous demand

I make and make again
to hear the whole story,
heart's own Yiddish, nothing lost.

104.

Be quick continuous
as heart is music
no repeats, only once

this music is, from first tone to endless end,
that better Mozart they call silence
leaving all your clothes behind

with all your heart
run in moonlight for your life
the blue thing time ends.

105.

It's hard not to see
every thing as a map of something else,
and only romantics when they look

deep into the eyes of some other one suppose
the map they read is of the land below—
every land flies some other country's flag

and the map I offer you all unwitting
is of another place entirely
Sohio road map of Indiana for '67

you try to find me and all you find
are sand dunes by the lake, Michigan City,
a prisoner dying in the electric chair

the scream of official murder
never leaves the wounded air
and you can hear him in my face.

106.

A strange man calls to her from the shore
but she is a girl, she likes what girls like,
the chapel is darker than a river

no chance of answering
back, answering a word eaten by moths
but the moths fly out when you think it.

107.

All the people you find when you walk in
saying language but not praying
and not one of them you ever knew

and now they all are almost you.
Sophia, asking for it,
to need it, to demand it of you,

what we ask for
is not what we desire said Lacan, but she
means it, she has a house

where it is so, you need to know
that seven I-beams hold it up
the rock she built on

she stands on what is
firmest in you when you press in
otherwise wisdom

just a bag of tricks
just a book born from a book
or mostly a dream forgot on waking

carrier wave a sine
and certain blue invariants wake you
at their season

we call them *fiori*,
the flowers of mathematics
he said we call them flowers

but I: what kind? do you have Persian roses,
gold nasturtiums with twisted beaks and good to eat,
pink hollyhocks like tipsy sentinels,

which? But he: no names please, these
are flowers that grow where colors come from
don't sweat the vocabulary, abstract blooms. But I *do*,

hate you if I can't smell your jasmine,
sometimes the tree of mind is a dead tree
core rotten, ready to fall, but like yew trees grow from the
    outside in

and live again, the outside makes the inside,
hate you if I can't hold your name in my mouth
I came here for the vocabulary

that is my tribe I came to save and be saved by,
not the dreary suburbs of arithmetic,
disguised as sculpture carved from emptiness.

108.

So what does go on inside a stone?
Repentance. *Om Vajrasattva*
samaya the chemistry begins,

what philosophers call Being
is a long purification.
An earlier occasion wakes in this.

No wonder they call it rock,
it sinks down inside itself and tries
to obliterate the ancient difference

heal me of my music,
re-pot the sansevieria,
call the plumber, answer her letter,

I am all that is aloud
he said, and saying makes me so
so I make sound,

I am clamor in the courtyard
like cars or camels, market, cathedral,
they don't know what they sell or why they buy

all we really need is take
this from my hand and give me what's in yours,
that sort of stone,

the water droplets in these clouds
all come from *aion*
the cerebro-spinal fluid of everywhere

faucet common earth swims in it
water of the wise our ordinariest
I tasted your tears.

I became your child.

109.

Cambered. Bent off a berm
the bad road comforts
goes away from what only you can do

into the field of pretty people
who can all do sort of anything
but the forgiveness begins

your silence silences me
not this life but some other
how many times has this letter been read

The unforgivingly tacit.
Don't shut up at me. How loud a touch.
Look my hand up in your dictionary.

See what it means by touching you
or this leaf it lifts
from the forest floor of an old poem no one reads

even the one who holds it takes
only that leaf
from all those trees.

Each beast is a manner knowing,
each animal is a priest of a different god,
and all the gods are also priests

who try to worship Something Else
sunlight on the lawn
or almost lost in trees

sought at midnight behind your eyes
keeps saying your particular prayers
amber light and broken wall

if you have a you to hold me in.
The law was made for humankind
but the human was made for the word

word from which a law was woven
words to unspeak words
unpronounce the silence.

A dog is always trying to blurt out the word
its master means
(pit bull; 'Sunday in the Park'

'the language!') unpronounced
the silence, the unforgivable
silence, neglect, dumb wedding.

Loki led me all the way and left me
woke and looked at me and slept
and I became his dream,

and way down Tuesday I was born
and he dreams all my calendar and you
shake it till he wakes and lets me loose

dreamless in detail abhorrently free,
no dignity but desire
he said and the leaf split in nervous fingers

light showed through o you you're always
coming back you never get there
there would be here once I am.

Smash his mirror, the car still floats
over the silent orchestra, the girl in tights
will never reappear from the magician's cabinet—

what's gone is gone, and that's all that comfort is.

110.

no more measure than ivy on a wall
the image of the goddess appeared to her at the base of
   the tree   *Drolma*
all white, portending long life

and what life is made of
a necklace of intimate awarenesses
spaced in healing silence

we have seen
too many images she says,
now look at me and fail to see,

now be the light the other side of seeing,
furrow running deep through time
now let me lick the seeing from your eyes.

111.

How to live
without hope
the minister

in empty logging truck
his virgin bride
entering the forest

the trees
are made of wood, the sky
is made of god

that's all he knows.
She sleeps beside him,
someday everything

will be everything
again but not now.
Now is for driving

rig empty
into the forest
not even praying

what kind of prayers
anyhow can trees
understand?

Wisdom begins where blame ends.
Hope hides
the place you stand.

112.

You and your castle in the Highlands
you and your ink in my pen
you and the bright red blue and green and yellow toy truck

size of a real logging rig he drove it
he was a minister married—do they get married?—
to his child bride all through the mountains, Aux Arcs,

down where the rainbows are, truck always empty
never a log or load in it
empty as a rainbow

but still they survived, didn't quarrel,
she was too young to have rights, he too sad
to want anything, they got there and were gone again,

only the colors were certain; with the sorrow,
the green landlocked sorrow of the place,
how we let things just happen and happen

till there is nowhere to go
but it was a dream darling only a dream
yes but why do we let dreams happen

why don't we break into the engine room
like when I was five and could drive the whole house
motorman it through the world

my hand on the throttle of the furnace room door
why don't we take charge of the dream
and make it go where we need to be

with robins singing and why is the dream so sad
because the man has studied the blue mirror
till all the clouds fell into his mind.

Then tell me love how this is part of that
and these and those of this one thing
one taste arisen from all your wheat

you milk the cow all some all same
so that one skin holds all this in?
How have the many become one

and one become someone
just like a song ending
and a comfortable silence *reigns*

they used to say, comfort of things lost
comfort of never being there again
the castle on the rock, the king your ancestor

stumbling murdered to his bed,
poor land, poor people, all he has to learn
and he has one long night to learn it in

how is this death different from my last?

113.

Shadows of fingers
have oil on them the language falls
two men try to walk into each other

one more blessed language
coos in a stranger's throat
did I ever tell you how I like your shape

the special equations of your slope
in those days I still knew numbers
now there are no creatures in those trees

or only one and the forest is still there
break a lance in broken land
blue fountains overflow with shriek

a maiden-in-peril is just that form of a dragon
the beast displays like a peacock's tail
to inveigle knights with other commitments

to rescue her by kissing it
uncanny marriage
move into the cave and spend her gold

read scripture in the evening of a warm day
but what kind of bible is that spread on your knees
you read with your hands

the way in my home town men talked in the market
running your fingers over every page
until the soft-throated book begins to speak:

In the endings a woman unmade
the skies and earths you thought you had
and it is always the first day

the rest of the text becomes the mind you read it with
Are you the devil, dragon? I am Eve
she said, what Adam thought a snake was my long arm

lifting actual substance from the empty tree
he took it from my fingertips
and nibbled, I felt his teeth close soft on flesh and fruit

and I knew at last the old thing was undone
and he was ready for the first day again
this day in my hand now to your eyes bring.

114.

Agincourt. So many battles to remember,
salt on the girl's tail to make her stay,
obsolescent tendernesses when we were flesh.

Borodino, strange rippling effects blood in sunlight,
officers fall from their horses crushing
pedestrian uhlans with friendly gravity,

Crecy, I loved you once, smug as a poem,
a balladeer with a pike through his chest,
his song comes back to the heart like a letter with the
    wrong address,

Dunkirk, or addressed to a dead man
in a burnt down house, escape while you can
from the entanglements of feeling by fleeing

Evesham Moor, vague purple glow
comes over me when I remember
I am in trouble now, a name sticks like tar, one single
    dead man

Flodden Field, I fall for all the music
incessant noonday marriages and count the corpses
all human love is incest, love is famously like war

Gettysburg, both afflictions of the soul arise from anxiety
and swelter through the ordinary landscape charging
    through the fire
and never a city to stop us, fields of fat crows,

Helgoland not all the seas can put the fires out,
rocky island where the dead come to live
civility is the highest virtue since from it all others come

Inkerman, the ill-clad troops, the anguish
of another language caught inside our clothes
the wounds walk towards me asking me to lick them closed

Jena, love is an intellectual riding down the street
on an ill-tamed horse, a glimpse in her window
and down he goes on cobblestones, trampled by his own,

Khartoum, a massacre mostly, her postcard read,
the ancient leavings of the heart's desire
indifferented in yellow sand, dead before ink-dry

Lucknow, there is no hiding place, no brick
to close the gaps in our poor walls
through which the rebels pour or we see a woman walk
    serene apart,

Maldon, from the sea they come to swamp us
murder is just one more feeling, an island soul
holds hard, a hand, the little things we die for

Namur, how ridiculous I am, my ravelin and turret,
    my fortress
any teenage rainstorm can overwhelm, great glacis
spread out in glistening sunlight, love lies down to die

Omagh, I was there, can't tell the lovers from the loathers
summer cold and winter clement, a randy valley
with too many daughters, no end to strife ever,

Pharsalus, the anonymity of flesh, dead
or dying, desired or desiring, the liturgy of blood,
kings change crowns above the corpses

Québec a defender dead among his defeated soldiers
a rose still in his teeth a kiss we recollect a word we weep
    to remember
up steep streets the raving winners barf their way

Ruhr ruins us all the bombed machinery
all hope and no have, all have and no hope
a million workers stuck inside a single job

Stalingrad, all snowjob and surrender,
all horror laid aside I phone again and again
until the answerless court martial decides she isn't home

Trenton, it's never glamorous, it always loses
you can't stop it, it's like a bridge with no turning
something starts it and you're hopelessly estranged

Ulm, from what is your own, my own become another's,
a steeple sticks into the sky, every place we are is Babel,
love flies from any room into the dark where war is waiting

Venus and Mars always together, always in trouble,
illegal, eternal, minds meant for each other,
Turks and courtesans die in fields outside Vienna,

Waterloo, in mud, Freud called it, mud of mind
below the feelings, the psyche stuff, the beautiful
wrong explanations, to desire is already to be defeated,

Xanthos, river like her hair you see it so
all the old books are young in her
all the gods fight with each other and she smiles uncertain,

Ypres, they thought at first it was poetry to fight, this word-
soaked blood and shit, this love
affair with other people's private parts the body is,

Zululand, love makes a colony of the other
and rules it till rebellion ruins both,
the same blood that rose to love you spills in shame.

115.

On the other side
I have invented
a new number

Which one is that?
I made up three
and any three before

me meant something
else, my three is this
and who are you?

I am Two the fairy
said and I sleep
in the lines of your palm

numberless and neat
no one now alive
can tell making up

from finding out
and you're no exception
you are the rule.

116.

So we went to the featureless hotel
and bit each other by the window
till it was suppertime on earth

a grey thing happened to the air
the desk clerk smiled like a passing freight
recommended we eat Korea or Vietnam

we dined on their unconquered meat
fish from their persistent streams wise pools
what is this wisdom that comes from defeat

Wirtschaftswunder, an argument
only has to last through dinner
green tea ice cream and then

the normal desperation can begin
to find a taxi to take us to
a place we do not know how to be

I am the analyst you are the bed
between us a person must one day rise
or already subsist, the Missing Think

we'll call it, the miracle
of what you really mean
lying there flat as a dollar bill

thinking your father dreaming your mother
and all your hundred thousand brothers
beat you with their little sticks

till I am nothing but a question mark
curled over you to taste and tell
every question is a circle left unclosed.

117.

Now he was a sailor who had been a priest
who knew the winds and what they said
who knew the land the ocean tended to

in other words he knew the name of the day itself
and why the moon was red last night
turf fire dying in a grate of cloud

and night was just learning too
truth was sleeping in her book
and interesting animals prowled suburban lawns

and the moon was on fire
just like the Bible or the sea
the terrible contradiction we call skin

what keeps me from you lets me touch you
questionless answer
a cloud built into the mind

Go already to the Italy that calls you
no happening happens here no willows,
you don't have to need anything

sometimes not to hear is best
and never listen, let the crows
pay such attention for you

but there is no such, nothing but this,
and fools strum guitars in distant gardens
strange walls with quince trees you fall in love

no place like this place, fierce without resemblance,
commas hurtling through a wordless text
crows, he said,

we saw them, we were in love with other people,
the phone rang, the mail came, rain fell
what could be more natural,

a nursemaid spanking a child, o woods
o solitarinesse, he cried, if ever a bird could
you could and then be there aloud

trembling on the brink of music
but still just trying to breathe—
du calme! look at the colors alone

ignore the shapes from which they rise and fall.

118.

Not push the trees
not suck the wind
alabaster fountain's broken

from purl of water lone
don't breathe a bird in
when you bellow forget the colors

hold on to the old bread
once I drank the sea I thought I could
and woke up in or as America

coiled in my ancestor's loins
a specter of the future
a self without a land

it is death for a soul to be west
he said and the burning chapel
never goes out, the Mass they're chanting there

never finishes, the lover who was once a knight
is a priest now, he sings it,
missa cantata, Low Mass chanted by one priest

and Mrs Grimaldi pays every week
to hear that music
to bring her dead son home from the war

and all the people shamble to communion
in organ Mascagni's intermezzo
we all are caught by music

that strange circumcision of the mind
doing something to the body to mark the soul
a negative tattoo, an Absence Duly Noted

because the One we worship is missing too,
lost foreskin of the universe,
the hooded comforter, the incurable healer,

we worship a god who has lost even his image
a god from the formless realm
who teaches us to scoff at idols

images, snapshots of the momentary real,
beware of pictures
because we fall in love with everything we see.

119.

Horn call knows a hand to hold
old woods of Europe oak or beech
tribes drifting through ghost malls and cathedrals

the color of the moon has changed
the taste of wine is not the same
so many cans of fish you open now are empty

not even the sound of the sea
when you hold them to your ear
just the quiet gleam of metal anodized

but the trees are loud
creak like trombones in little wind
creatures whose ontological status you tend to doubt

they are all around you now
visible almost, moving like the bright shadows of
    dark things,
augments of transparency

some of them talk, Have you paid
for your language, lady?
Have you bent to taste the red water

flowing from the holy well, chalybeate,
this little rill will lead you to the place,
a place like a person, a person waiting for you

all this in horn call hear
rosary beads for atheists
the dream mistunes the day

la scordatura

there, that's what it means
every state of awareness calls
every other into question—look

we can do it that way too, neither,
nor, more, some, all
differences in sheer difference solved,

the logic of emptiness
I know who I am it doesn't
matter if you doubt

I will be you what you need
you be the airplane I'll be the sky
pressed to the lamppost I'll close my eyes

until everyone alive has run to hide
now only the ontologies are left
raw naked roaring in the trees

now say your prayers
a hunk of amber up your stairs
where Wisdom waits smoking in emptiness

because we happen to be living we see her as a woman
Sophia, Maria, Magdalena, *yeshe*,
a roaring silence in the small blue sky inside one
    more flower.

120.

Majesty is born of self-analysis
the king has no body of his own
only the queen connects him with the sky

as he her to this earth
he said, and I laughed at the inversion
even as my silver slipper trod

light the azure carpet rising
and we were lungs together
in faith's old hospital—you

could never say a word I don't believe
and that is our intimate self-deception
shared, two men passing on a road at night

a place where unseen to them a dead animal
—deer, raccoon, opossum—rots
and each man thinks the stink comes from the other.

And so we share the kingship of all things
each supposing himself amazingly afflicted
whereas, whereas … here

the orator began to stammer, the poem
faltered over breakfast, a bile taste
which had the shape of silence rose

no he said there are no kings
there is only a personless ascension
summer-heavy, a dry bone's fresh tune.

121.

Memory is like that,
a taste in the mouth,
raptacious, a spasm

from almost another universe,
the quick talons seize
and the hawk's up there again

with the astonished sparrow snatched
struggling not to be remembered
but there she is after all, her eyes closing

and I am passive in this theater
blameless pelvis
where all this old blood pours out still

one word then another
till a man or woman
stands complete

incarnate, created in memoria,
old albatross, the giant
wooden elephant in Margate.

My mother in a rowboat looks up from the Monticello news.

122.

Wise about everything but your life
you finally remember a grove
of tall pines on the road to Callicoon

bare floor of such forests
your shadow walking in front of you
longer and longer till it disappears in the dark—

sunset and all the world's behind you now
birds have mostly given up by now
but a few linger near you

making their usual wise remarks
you understand for once, your life
is just a part of earth's weather,

doesn't matter much, no more than rain
says one and another: going
is all you're good at, so go

so you go forward, when day comes
you go beyond the day
and mountains, you go beyond the mountains

and you are here now at last
you have come to the place
where your shadow finds you again.

123.

What does the inside look like
of anything I mean
not just you or me,

the word once heard
of any system, processing unit,
piece of wood, bird song, self.

What does it look like
and what does it say,
I have been listening to it all my life

you light a candle for your forgetting
and touch me—whole forests
roll up close, with bears and wolves in them,

my brothers, fallen towers half rise up
and owls bother them all night with music
all round me the fable spreads out for your touch

Grail and maiden castle horn call in lost valley
dragons pretending to be our sleep
till then it changes.

Everything does.
A muscle moves inside an old sack
and the Wheat Wife comes out,

blond and pretty, with sticky fingers.
The mill collapses, sluiceway overflows.
And she touches me too.

124.

There is a certain place in the woods
I have to keep my eye on
to be true to myself and the leaf

the way the sun speaks into it
small almost furtive
sentences of light,

there is a door there
open for me, only for me
only there, something coming

only that place, only by looking
never by seeing, only
the way the light alights there

only the way the light lets me,
slow writhing of sun dapple
on the already luminous shadow forest floor

not to flounder vaguely
towards the propositional, just watch it
what else are hearts for?

We speak by keeping silent,
silence is a method, a machine,
a constant presence, a conversation,

a muscle, a melody, a friend.

125.

This rain that isn't
today, this language
that does not represent

and thus is sacred, aniconic
language, a unicorn
you can't see, in woods

cut down before you were born,
a language saying everything
and showing nothing,

tell and don't show
saves us from *Hell*,
where all the images wind up

where stored in the dark
they do their cruel work
where in the dark *they* remember you.

126.

When the near is ending
and the air is close but everything else is far,
he gets paranoid about weather,

about Israel and Christians
questing the red heifer
he remembers Arabia

where *Damcar* the City
of the Blood of the Lamb
lived once, a hidden place

in the Hadramaut
he'd seen it only once,
they wouldn't talk to him,

they pretended to be stones
they pretended he was just some light
or shadow falling on them.

The conspiracy of silence
silenced him as usual, the sullen
angry father of the world

mortifying his son.
Each of us his only son.
There is a language though

where all this is not so,
a language that lets you go—
if he could learn it he would be free,

a mask out of time in the nick of time,
when he was little
he thought it was Greek

and Greek had traces of it
that other language,
not the 'original' speech

but the final one, the one
they all aim at, where all
the other languages converge

even now he hears it sometimes
already, falling asleep
people talking just outside the morning door.

127.

There isn't a single flower
that doesn't know your name
doesn't jabber it inside your bones

alas when you just glance that way
not even wishing,
there is no little world here,

a few churches, a couple of girls
in white satin blouses too heavy
for the August night, the crowd

and the fields at morning
empty as Easter—
how little I've given you after all

when I meant to give you rubies,
at least in these woods we hear
not far off rush hour traffic

at least I can help you remember
some of the names of what you want
some of the people you have been

and maybe that is a kind of help
like a door left open behind me
when I finally shoulder through the tender wall.

128.

Moment a mountain
and long to climb
a song of gibberish

in my lips, a school of it
to sing just the sounds
in your ears the words

left long ago, the sounds
are shadow sounds,
the school of midnight

licks your ears,
or this sweet broken limestone track
the humid path among the maples

the dreary company of hope
shuffling vaguely towards the wisdom temple
and then the quiet eyes of the finders

gleam with kindness there
you are a finder
and we are fathers of a minute

children of fake memories
and all we ever really have is skin,
the Differencer, the gonfalon,

the sacred colors of my House
tattered in cathedral gloom
or my youngest hand athwart your spine.

Something like that. Everything over
now, a bull slain on a stone
finally the blood comes home.

Something like this: the anthem
that is also a dissertation
a midrash on this moment

this unexplored galaxy you call Now
vanishes into the breath but you can go
chase it at right angles to time present

sail by cosine out into the actual
long as you like, after one whole breath
and before another, the light place in between,

some die there like Scott in wordless snow
or come back home with hard gospels
everybody credits but nobody practices,

breathe, for breath
is my path and skin my continent,
the two modalities of mastery between.

So I asked my teacher: Do I have it straight
and he: fragments of the miracle
cling here and there to your remarks

but on the whole the thing you speak lacks tune.

129.

The remembering
is no different from wanting
for desire is the fuel of thinking

and by its lust
connects all things perceived
into the web I call 'my life'

this silly reminiscence
of what I thought was me
was only shadows of

a genuine identity.
Guess, and guess again.
Energy, the work inside,

the saints called it devilish,
the inner person with whom
the outer had to reckon

but the only alternative
is to be me.
Bloody family of the pronouns

smell of ammonia, smell
of horse manure, old wagon
full of cauliflower

my father said That
is a whiffletree
my mother said nothing

and I have been Jewish ever since.

130.

Enough left in the empty bottle
to drink the dust of light.
Morandi's grey paintings.

I get sorry when I think of you
how I will never taste
the milk inside your basin

no wind stirs the curtains.

131.

I know nothing
and this nothing that I know
I learned it from a book.

Is it the same nothing you know
dear friend
so far across the straits of distance?

Hills like clouds are promises
no one believes.
Come soon so I can know

your nothing too.

132.

Conundrum: what
is like a cave what is a ruby
I heard her thinking

in the core of the apple
after I had eaten all the rest
there was a cave at the beginning

seedless as bananas our time
was white inside with afternoons
a jungle a channel

through thick trees ancient stonework
underfoot, the testimony
zakhor the predecessors, who?

I was a radio back then
I could talk but not show myself
now a wolf, all teeth and meanings

and nothing told
unless you call what you hear
when you listen hard to my breath

some kind of story
clear water moving
swift below the frozen stream.